WORD ETCHINGS

Glenn Lumb

CHAS CANN PUBLISHERS

Copyright © 2023 Glenn Lumb

All rights reserved.

This book is sold subject to the condition that it shall not, by way of trade or otherwise, be lent, resold, hired out, or otherwise circulated without the publisher's prior consent in any form of binding or cover other than that in which it is published and without a similar condition, including this condition, being imposed on the subsequent purchaser

Contents

Introduction		XII
1.	A Long Sentence	1
2.	A Stranger in Town	4
3.	Acne Academy	7
4.	Acquaintance	10
5.	Adhesion	12
6.	Adrift	15
7.	Ant Bashing	18
8.	Autumnal Skies	20
9.	Beauty and You	24
10.	Bed-Bugs Boogie	26
11.	Binge-Drinking	28
12.	Birthdays	31
13.	Bonnie and Clyde	34

14.	Bouncing Brenda	37
15.	Bubble of Love	39
16.	Bullets and Bombs	41
17.	Canine Conclusion	43
18.	Celtic Wildlife Gig	45
19.	Chemotherapy Combat	48
20.	Coldest of Dreams	50
21.	Colonel Covid's Memoirs	52
22.	Colour	54
23.	Company Man	56
24.	Condiments	59
25.	Consolation Wine	60
26.	Contentment and the Ferryman	62
27.	Cosmic Conclusion	65
28.	Curtains	67
29.	Daffodils	69
30.	Dancing Dougie	71
31.	Demise	74
32.	Diary of a Distant Dormouse	76
33.	Edith	78
34.	Egg Head	81

35.	Everlasting Allies	85
36.	Family Outing	89
37.	Farmyard Comedian	91
38.	Figure Of Eight	94
39.	Finger Licks and Card Tricks	96
40.	Flight of the Helium Balloon	98
41.	Frostie the Doughman	100
42.	Girlfriend	103
43.	Glass Ballerina	105
44.	Granite	107
45.	Hallelujah	109
46.	Hay Lay	112
47.	Her Majesty's Pleasure Deterrent	115
48.	Hokey Cokey Voting	118
49.	Hospital Patience	121
50.	Irish Incident	124
51.	Jolly Folly	128
52.	Junkie Astronaut	130
53.	King and Queen Festival	132
54.	Lather In Love	135
55.	Lucifer	137

56.	Malice of The Deer Hunter	139
57.	Maritime Myth	141
58.	O.T.T	143
59.	Penny For the Guy	145
60.	Plastic Love	147
61.	Psychic Sandman	148
62.	Pursuit of Positivity	150
63.	Rainbow Dream	152
64.	Ruby and my Rabbit	154
65.	Sandlewood Secondary Modern School and the Comic Strip Gate-Crasher	156
66.	Serenity	159
67.	Sixties Child	163
68.	Smokin` Roy and the Bad Boys	166
69.	Soul-Singer	171
70.	Spanish Flair	175
71.	Spider Rant	177
72.	Spite of the Night Dreamweaver	180
73.	Sugar Rush	182
74.	Swagger Fly	184
75.	Tale of a Pregnant Teapot	186
76.	Talons and Talents	188

77.	Teddy Bear Story	190
78.	The Adventures of Cartoon Boy	192
79.	The Annual Doggie Dinner Dance	194
80.	The Art of a Cunning Lyricist	196
81.	The Belly-Button Tree	198
82.	The Bonnie Bauble Affair	200
83.	The Chemotherapy Cavalry	204
84.	The Coughalot Club	206
85.	The Floral Sacrifice	210
86.	The Forest of Dreams	212
87.	The Home-Town Rats	214
88.	The Honeybee-Buzz	217
89.	The Pope	218
90.	The Silent Cemetery	219
91.	The Welcomed Arrival of Spring	223
92.	Toy-Box Scenario	225
93.	Tremor	228
94.	Two Stars out of Six	230
95.	War of Words	232
96.	Water Baby	234
97.	Wedding Day	236

98. White Stick	239
99. Winter Wonder	242
100. Your Spoken Words	244
Afterword	246

About the Author

The time has come for a change in life and in my case the change happens to be in actually releasing my collection of poems to the public as opposed to keeping them stashed away on my mobile. Writing them has been a therapeutic experience therefore one I wish to share in the hope the reader enjoys the journey along the way! No fancy stuff here! Just an amalgamation of random thoughts jotted down to conjure imagination and entice the brain with rhyme!

Please feel free to wander in and out of the various moods and attitudes on offer in the verses…go for it haha! A special mention for my extremely patient French Bulldog Cassie who has had to stand on street corners and in parks on many occasions while I tap out a few lines of prose on my phone!

To my son and daughter, namely, Aaron and Charlotte!
Love you lots! xx

Introduction

***

A moment to cherish,
An occasion to treasure,
Poems of privacy
Public forever,
Liberated, fated
For criticism,
Created in a state
Of optimism,
Hoping for a grade
Of overall approval
From intrigued readers
Pleased and jovial,
Happy to lose themselves
In my prose,
Mission accomplished?
Who knows!

***

A Long Sentence

***

The place is closed down now,
Not in my dream,
A prison, an island; captivity,
If I had powers
As with the Red Sea
I'd part the waves
And walk free!

Far from innocent,
I cannot pretend,
I'd ended the lives
Of innocent men,
Forsaken them, taken them
From next of kin,
An unforgivable sin!

Guilty of crimes,
Locked up with the bad,
Resigned to confines
Of Alcatraz,
Prisoners denied privileges,
The existence is drab,
A sentence to serve,
Deserved but sad!

In the cell next to me;
Al Capone,

Flexing his muscles
To ensure they're toned,
Mumbling something,
Sat on his own,
Private conversation,
Thoughts unknown!

George 'Machine Gun' Kelly
Waves a finger at me,
The intimidation I'm facing
Burns more than third-degree,
Feeling riddled with bullets
I'm a target that bleeds,
Condemned to suffer daily
With those guilty!

Robert Franklin Stroud;
The Bird Man of Alcatraz
Was not permitted to cater for birds
Despite those he had had,
His request while inside
Was bluntly denied;
The end of a feathered fad!

Corrosion, erosion,
The result of being exposed
To salt, sea air, the atmosphere
Led to the prison's close,
The colossal cost of shipping
Daily deliveries of food
Added to the decision
To make the move!

I cannot sleep; this bed's too hard,

Too bad it's all I've got,
A blanket, thin, inadequate,
It's essential wearing socks,
I've banged my head,
It hurts a bit,
Not used to sudden shocks,
I'm on the floor, out of bed,
Awake, my thoughts in knots;
Why did I dream of Alcatraz?
The reason has me foxed!

A Stranger in Town

***

Covering his head with a ten-gallon hat,
Swatting a fly off his nose,
A neckerchief worn like a loose cravat
As he stands in dirt-stained clothes,
Leading his horse to a water trough
For a well-earned, satisfying drink,
A stranger in town, suspicions aroused,
Who knows what the townsfolk think!

A room, a bath in some foisty hotel
To wash the long journey away,
Miles of sweat that congeals, infests
When left forms its own decay,
A man might be or feel penniless
When submerged in a tub of suds
After riding a trail through sun-soaked days
Feels he's more than rich enough!

Stepping into the crowded saloon bar,
Doors swinging as he pushes on through,
Loud singing from drunken cowboys
As whisky flows with the brew,
'Gonna buy a sweet girl a drink mister?'
He looks at her flimsy, lace dress,
'Not today ma'am even though you have
An impressive pair of breasts!'

In strolls the sheriff with star-shaped badge,
Word had spread around,
A dapple-grey mare has mysteriously appeared
Together with a stranger in town,
'Where're you heading boy?' the sheriff stands poised,
His deputy looking real hard,
Our cowboy takes a deep breath, says,
'Right now, I'm heading for the bar!'

Heads turn, eyes burn, hearts in mouths,
Is double-trouble suddenly arising?
The sheriff and his deputy convinced this 'celebrity'
Should be heading over the horizon,
'You'd better come with us, don't make a fuss,
We don't trust you mooching around!',
'Why, what have I done?'
'Nothing son! but you're a stranger in town!'

They march him to his dapple horse,
Ensure his gun's not loaded,
He only came in for a drink
Although you'd never know it,
The west is wild in retrospect,
Acceptance is quite rare,
A stranger in town creates more frowns
Whenever one appears!

Are you aiming to pursue a trail
On a cowboy adventure quest,
Wear the traditional outfit
A cowboy would out west?
Be thick-skinned as Indians
May want to claim your scalp,
Avoid the town called 'Hostile';

It wouldn't be any help!

***

Acne Academy

***

Principal Pimple sat upright
Upon the subject's nose,
A whitehead plain for all to see
In a splendid pus-filled pose,
A herd of zits surround him,
Spread across the face,
Not a bad lot, good in spots,
Mocked by the human race!

"I relish every one of you!"
Principal Pimple told his clan,
Bursting to make an impression,
Spreading acne all they can,
"We need to increase in numbers,
Greasy skin is such a blessing,
They itch, scratch bellies and backs,
Split zits when undressing!"

A rash had settled on the chin,
"Welcome!" cried the zits,
"Attention will be drawn to you
If symptoms persist!"
Sunrays through a window pane
Overheat the skin,
Zits are mini volcanoes
That expel the mass within!

Principal Pimple felt the pressure
Of two thumbs that were applied,
A pair of nails pressing
To eject his insides,
Heavily protesting,
Refusing to surrender
He braced himself to save himself
From a yellow pus dilemma!

The zits looked up, admired him,
Red raw from the attempt
To eliminate him from the face
He did not compliment,
What a great example
For zits to learn the art
Of resisting any pressure
To split them all in half!

Creams, antiseptic lotions,
Potions closely linked,
Applied daily but failing
To make picked zits extinct,
Cures to cleanse the pores of gunge
Are met with criticism,
Not always successful
In a facial exorcism!

Confident zits happily sit
On faces proud as punch,
Encourage second glances
From those put off their lunch,
Spotty blotches discourage
Physical attraction,
Who wants to kiss a face with zits?

It's the easiest way to catch them!

Large spots, small spots,
Blemishes, cold sores,
Relishing the prospect
Of blocking up the pores,
Schools of spots and pimples
Graduate to a degree,
Attending class, achieving a 'pass'
At the Acne Academy!

Acquaintance

***

You ask for trouble in all that you do;
Alligator wrestling in crocodile shoes,
Condemning bombs then detonating the fuse
With your explosive views!

You invent complications (confuse the plot),
Downing Red Bull in a china shop,
Your watery eyes wet from peeling shallots;
Fake tear drops!

A challenging road dictates a rough ride,
Driven to despair, overtaken by pride,
Accidents happen; we all slip & slide,
Words collide!

Your vocation lays in creating a fuss,
Our solid foundation; reduced to dust!
There's danger in blatantly betraying a trust:
All faith is lost!

Words from your mouth leave a bitter taste,
A dual personality, sadly two-faced,
Your ego is massaged, inflated, embraced;
Head case!

It ends in a muddle whatever you try;
Bungee-jumping in a gale force 9,

Calling someone a pig although they're a swine;
Disgruntled friend of mine!

Adhesion!

***

Don't try to free them
Let the adhesion
Which holds them strong and firm
Be a permanent bond
For whenever it's gone
Is difficult to return,
Any love is good love,
Good enough to save from ruin,
Whatever the scale, firm or frail
It's certainly worth pursuing!

Why tease them
Let the adhesion
Keep them held together,
They have a head start
Why pull them apart
As their lives are getting better?
They're solidified as a pairing;
A 'two in one endeavour',
A unit, an item, presumed the right one,
To savour not to sever!

Jealousy
Brings negativity
Incited by spiteful minds,
The sort that approves of others' bad moods,
Relishing in their decline,

Impelling their `one upmanship`
To benefit personal pride,
Unhappy till their target is
Satisfactorily jeopardized!

Good wishes
Are traditional,
Crucial for success,
Partnerships progress
When void of undue stress,
It's quaint to see the intimacy
Where no-one seems hard pressed,
An acceptance, no rivalry
Or hint of competitiveness!

Let love flourish
Not be discouraged,
Encouragement is a must,
Young or old, twofold
They control their mutual trust,
Couples together is a pleasure,
The combination is a plus,
What they have embellishes
The love in all of us!

Too many relations folding,
Not upholding
The test of time,
After scaling the rungs, failing
To complete the higher climb,
Stopping during the walk, the thought
Of going that extra mile,
Doubts are precautionary measures
When pressured by denial!

Win some, lose some,
Don't deny or refuse them,
`Twosomes` are better than one,
A friend in need is a friend indeed
(An anticlimax to be shunned),
Stopping sobbing halves the problem,
Mere tears are overcome,
Sympathy has an intricacy
Believed to be second to none!

Every feasible reason
Would allow adhesion
Between a courting couple,
Some find the need to intervene,
Cause disruptive trouble,
Shallow minded people
Being far from subtle,
Let adhesion bond them so no-one
Can burst their bubble!

Adrift!

***

She stands on the pier,
Wind ruffling her hair,
Looking out to the distant horizon,
Lost in thoughts of a personal sort
Where emotions tend to rise in,
She and debris, drifting away
In depths where ships capsize in.

She lives on the coast,
A location she chose,
Alone after three broken marriages,
Her parents long gone, an emigrated son,
Several affairs with odd characters,
One was a sailor, daydreaming behaviour;
Reminiscing her time with the mariner.

Thoughtful walks on the beach,
Other possibilities,
Will her life of loneliness ever change?
If so, what direction,
Love and affection
Or isolation with age?
Intrigue, personal needs,
Another autobiography page.

Deep concentration,
Her mind racing,

A turning point in her aims,
A positive attitude
Is the way to improve
And capitalise on gains,
Determination despite frustration
Encourages the same,
She mulls things over constantly,
Mentally engaged.

Strolling through dunes,
Wisps of her perfume,
A solitary figure on the beach,
Tides come and go
Have an unrestricted flow,
She is free as these so to speak,
Kissed by sun on warmer days
The water's surface resonates,
Displays a scene of tranquillity
Quite unique.

She has beauty, charm, charisma,
Good looks to assist her,
A worthy catch, attractive to any male,
Her faith in passed relationships
Has affected her self-confidence,
Can she risk another one to fail?

Maybe, one day, the incentive
To find love reinvented,
Fate and fortune play a sensitive game,
Twists and turns in how we rate,
A slalom course to negotiate,
An emotional trip through pleasure
And the pain!

She stands on the pier
With a vacant stare,
December brings a northern, biting wind,
A lone figure in the chill,
Cold and vulnerable,
Watching the waves roll in,
There'll be warmer, relaxing days,
She'll feel settled in sun's rays,
A companion, an understanding;
Fulfilled!

Ant Bashing

***

The heatwave's
Been all the rage
Like it's going out of fashion,
It's the season for breeding,
Reproduction interactions,
Animals & insects,
Sexual action,
I'm on a mission in my kitchen;
Ant bashing!
Dozens of the blighters
Crawling, dashing,
Searching for crumbs
Or some form of
Saccharine,
Uninvited mites
Intending to fatten,
They all look the same,
Identically blackened!
Appearing from nowhere,
They're gone! then they're back again!
The only way
To delay them
Is blatantly flatten them!
Squashed by a finger
They don't know what's happening,
Wipe them all out
With a fatal battering,
They tack, zig zag,

Set your teeth chattering
In a frantic chase
Where your aim is to splatter them!
In this case no way you can
Blame ants for panicking,
Haphazardly running for life;
For sanctuary!
Endangered by failing
To escape inhumanity,
Threatening hygiene
And human vanity,
"Get out of my kitchen
Or face calamity!"

Left right! left right!
Here comes the ant patrol!
North ants, south ants,
Ants in your pants ants!
Ants in your pantry...........
Tenfold!!!

Autumnal Skies

***

Unsettled weather,
Storms on the rise,
The familiar presence;
Autumnal skies,
Dark, dirty clouds
In a gloomy ascent
Cast a drab shadow
Everywhere they descend,
Landscape discoloured,
Painted black and grey
Etched in a charcoal
Sketch of disarray,
Bare trees have shed leaves
Swept callously by the wind,
Dispersed with abandon,
A random scattering,
Wild animals take refuge
In the deluge taking place,
Scamper for shelter,
Anxious to escape,
The climate is hostile,
A snarling gale,
Atmospheric intimidation,
Spitting venom with rage,
A built-up frustration,
Bad-tempered rows,
Physical evidence
In shifting clouds,

Storms have no tolerance,
An arrogant streak,
A dictating impatience
Towards serenity,
It's startling displays
Amaze, so exciting,
The formidable duo;
Thunder and lightning
Performing a gig
On an overhead stage,
Strobe lighting, striking,
An alarming display,
Surround Sound technology,
Dramatic audio,
3D dimension
In full stereo,
Thunderclaps in unison,
Firecracker style,
Deafening impact,
Repetitive, wild,
Awe inspiring, tiring,
Feel it rumble away,
Relief, relaxation,
Sanity prevails!

Calm after the storm,
Tension subsides,
The horizon assigned to
Autumnal skies,
A pale cream background
Interrupted by trees,
Birds finding food,
A formation of geese
Flying high in the sky

On a mission somewhere
For a well-timed arrival
In survival warfare,
Silky otters tread water
Juggling with fish,
A kestrel hovers menacingly,
Endlessly famished,
Nervous deer grazing,
Alert to every sound,
The earth disturbed by wildlife,
Soil inhabited underground,
Bird-song, almost dormant,
Breeding season laid to rest,
Winter's booked a reservation
For its robin redbreast guest,
Earthworms serve as breakfast,
Insects crawl in moss,
Abandoned nests are visible
Where trees' leaves have fallen off,
Mud acknowledges the rainfall,
Drops from sodden thorns,
Wings bathing in the shallow depths;
Benefits of the storm,
Moisture hangs on spiders' webs,
Slides down slimy bark,
A splash as oak trees occasionally shed
Their acorns feet apart,
Dense mist descends mysteriously,
Visibility is scarce,
The sense of smell more crucial
If a predator appears,
The river runs its current,
A gentle, methodical flow,
Essential to many organisms

Living down below,
Bugs, beetles, water termites
Solve appetites of frogs,
Toads expose their throats like balloons,
Sing songs on vacant logs.
Nature is incredible,
An asset to all that survives,
Everything in this season sees pleasing
Autumnal skies!

Beauty and You

***

Spaghetti thin legs,
Smooth eggshell thighs,
A carrot complexion,
Beetroot eyes,
A cling-film top
(See-through surprise),
How could I resist
As you walked on by?

Chocolate-mousse hair,
Cherry dimpled cheeks,
That tic tac smile,
Peppermint teeth,
Milk blancmange skin,
Confectionery feet,
Soft, jelly bum,
Sweet, petite;
A sundae treat
Every day of the week!

Marzipan makeup,
Butter-cream face,
Liquorice mascara;
Impeccable taste!
Fondue foundation,
Wafer-thin waist,
Gelatine lip gloss;

Icing on the cake,
Full Monty facial,
Nothing half-baked!

A Wensleydale outlook,
Cheesy grin,
Fridge-cool presence;
Chilled out & in,
A cucumber face-pack
Cleanses the skin,
No Botox injections
Or suffering;
Beauty & you
Are identical twins!

Bed-Bugs Boogie

***

There's dry skin flaking in your bed,
You lie among the pile that's shed
And all those bugs among the sheets
Share your nights, the hours you sleep,
Never resting, digesting your sweat,
Infecting the pores in your stomach and chest,
Infesting your hygiene with surprising alarm,
A rising congestion of molesting harm,
Bugs spread viruses spurred by heat,
Generating pulsating, undesired in your sheets,
They feed on bacteria, delirious, 'on high',
A frantic batch of foul fungi,
Absorbing moisture, stalking your skin
Surfing your stomach; breathing out, breathing in,
Tucked in creases, overlaps of flesh,
Loving obesity, increasingly impressed,
An airbed of blubber, bouncy-castle glitz,
A free-for-all entanglement of parasites and nits,
Mixing, interacting, happy fungi-fools,
Party whooper-uppers seen by others as 'cool',
Dark shades for notoriety, their priority is fun,
Party-poopers get the usual kick in the bum,
Parasitic 'high-fives', pats on the back,
Groups of polluters in futile acts,
Enact naff diseases that seize any system,
Spread like measles, it's hard to resist them,
Miniscule mini-mites nibbling your toes,

(The foisty essence of cheese up the nose),
Ankle arbitrators absorbing the damp,
The icky, sticky substance that brings on pants,
Makes them gasp, shriek and groan,
Slurping your flesh down to the bone,
Nuzzling pimples, beauty-spots,
Guzzling perspired juicy drops,
Sucking flesh with lizard tongues,
Claw-like pincers hanging on,
Every deed performed by touch,
Irritation, skin is flushed,
Reddening from bedding mites,
Hotchpotch blotches; a dreadful sight,
Grazes, rashes, stinging cuts,
Willy abrasions, sucks on butts,
Scores of sores on body parts
Like indents on a board of darts,
Marks from sharp bites, bastard bugs
That take advantage when we're snug
And warm in blankets, snoring away
Oblivious to the bugs at play,
Swarming through mornings, awake at night,
Gnawing at soft spots, crawling for spite,
Giving us reason to wash and clean
But they remain despite hygiene.
As a footnote (though rather trite)
Try not to let the bed-bugs bite!

04 July 2019 17:06

Binge-Drinking

***

Binge-drinking
Got me thinking,
What a bloody jinx,
Throwing up in seconds
What took all night to drink,
Downing shots of vodka
Faster than the eye can blink,
"Hewing!" down the toilet,
Blocking up the sink,
Regurgitating liquid;
Alcohol excrement!
Pints of beer with frothy heads
Pee-weed in the Gents,
Delicate wine so refined;
Wine-bar supplement,
Okay in moderation,
A danger if the intent
Is to nullify the brain
Into bewilderment!

Binge-drinking,
Glasses chinking,
Never ending thirst,
Night clubs (the fight clubs)
Are seriously worse,
Open till the early hours
Licensed to serve,

Physical aggression
Unsettles the nerves,
Alcohol oppression
Depresses, disturbs,
Drunk girls in puddles
Lie huddled in kerbs,
Heads clutched in hands
Feeling like it will burst,
Their modesty lost
Knickers showing, raised skirts
Open to the theft of their
Mobile & purse!

Binge-drinking,
Raucous singing,
Dancing in the streets,
No favours to the neighbours;
Interrupted sleep,
Bottles flying, females crying,
Cut lips, broken teeth,
Paramedics curing headaches
Accompanied by police,
Arrests for drunken-disorder,
Failure to keep the peace,
A cup of tea in custody
Before delayed release!
Cooperation eliminates
A punishment increase,
A court date, a fine,
Don't expect a receipt,
Consequences, more intense
If there's a repeat!

Binge-drinking,

Sinking

Gallons of booze,
Abuse your livers
If that's what you choose,
Stay paralytic,
Keep friends amused,
It seems so pathetic,
What is there to prove
By swallowing so much
You can hardly move?
Falling down stairs
In inebriated mood,
I'm certain your
Ankles would disapprove
Being sprained or broken
Due to booze!
Binge-drinking is for losers;
Hope it's not you!

Birthdays

***

Birthdays come with age,
Celebrated when you're young,
Hearty parties thrown by parents,
Welcome everyone!
The blowing of the candles,
The "Happy Birthday!" song,
Rice Krispie cakes, souffles,
Jammy Dodgers, chocolate buns,
Jelly crammed with Smarties,
Ice-cream by the ton,
Musical chairs, mad scrambles, tears,
Cheers for seated bums,
Competition is tough, it's fisticuffs
Declaring who has won!

Kevin throws a tantrum,
Stamps on Jimmy's foot,
Holds him in a headlock
Learned from a wrestling book,
Jimmy grabs his dangleys
Gives them a mighty twist,
Fingers thrust up Jimmy's nose
Startle him a bit,
"Stop it now!" their mother's shout,
"Don't behave like childish kids!"
But that's exactly what they were
And exactly what they did!

In a circle, "pass the parcel",
Children hand it round,
Paper tearing, sharing
Sweets, treats that they have found,
Shirley Neemar looking meaner
Screaming out aloud,
"How is it I'm the only person
Left out in this crowd?"
She lifts a full-cream gateau
With a glaring, sneering frown,
Smashes it to smithereens
While jumping up and down!

Everyone's playing "statues",
"Did Rebecca move?"
Michael lost his footing
After stubbing his left toe,
Mary is hardly fairing
To stop scratching an itching nose,
Billy's staring upwards
Trying to look composed,
Is he in or is he out?
Debatable I suppose!
But Tom is out without a doubt
For shivering with a cold!

A hired clown entertaining,
Yellow shoes, floppy hat,
Shaping animals out of balloons;
A poodle, an overweight cat,
He does some slapstick movements,
Gets himself into a flap,
Trips over some legs, ending full length

Upon some lady's lap,
She shrieks, swings her handbag,
Giving him a whack,
"Slapstick comedy's funny,
You certainly fell for that!"

When the party games are over
The kids begin to leave,
Collected by their parents
Arriving randomly,
Party bags are handed out,
Cake slices well received,
Leftover buffet offered to
Those leaving hungrily,
"Thank yous" to the hostess
As a matter of courtesy,
Good manners taught to children
Are fulfilling from infancy,
Birthday boy keeps smiling,
A day of fun, frivolity,
One-year older, broader shoulders,
Five years from his teens!

Bonnie and Clyde

***

Let's creep out tonight,
Load up the van,
Ensure we're not seen by
Any woman or man,
Keep the lights off
Before the main road,
Let neighbour's sleep;
Comatose,
We have it all planned
As we take a ride,
We're a team; a mean-machine:
Bonnie & Clyde,
Setting out in secret
On a hard-core mission,
In pyjamas, balaclavas,
For a spot of fly-tipping,
There's a rusty gas oven
Rocking in the van
As we turn sharp corners
As fast as we can,
Bald car tyres,
A smashed ceramic sink,
A bicycle frame,
Loose chain, missing links,
A thinly-stuffed scarecrow
Having seen its day
Feeling only half

Of how it felt yesterday,
A ragged, dirty carpet
Folded in a heap,
Its underlay rotten,
Losing its physique,
Bricks and bags of rubble
Bouncing in the back,
Far too much trouble
To recycle; that's a fact,
A mouldy old lawn-mower;
Pitted blades, no wheels,
On its last, stained with grass,
Destined for some field,
We pull up in the countryside,
Fling open both back doors,
Drag stuff out to pile about
Without signs of remorse,
Flutters in the bushes,
Disturbed birds in the night
Wondering why the clatter
Of a vacuum-cleaner frights,
A mattress hits the ground with force,
A wardrobe on its way,
A dining-table with one leg,
Three chairs... hip hip hooray!
Further on we drop some more,
Laughing as we do,
This village we're in is such a dump
It seems to follow suit,
A fridge is toppled over,
Hits the ground... thud!
In a frigid position
Without a three-point plug,
Window-frames, glass smashing,

Crashes in the night,
Biffs and bashes clashing
As the naff trash falls from height,
Our cranky van is empty,
We flatter ourselves with pride,
On an illegal mission of suspicion,
Fly-tipping, Bonnie and Clyde!

13 December 2018 23:14

Bouncing Brenda

***

With her bedroom eyes, mattress thighs,
Duvet pupils twice the size,
Plumped up pillows, reddened face,
Erogenous zones in a private place
Grunts, groans, succulent licks,
Sticky belly-buttons, sweaty armpits,
'Oohs' and 'arrhs', sharp smacks that sting,
Bum-cheeks squeezed (a tease in the fling),
Huffs, puffs, roaming hands,
Calorie burning, frantic pants,
Bouncing Brenda lives the dream,
Shouts obscenities, bellowing screams,
Like a rodeo cowgirl; wild, Italian,
Bareback riding on a bucking stallion,
Waves an arm wildly circling in the air,
Letting out 'whoops' as a mating mare,
Horse sense, jump the fence, keep on high,
Don't stall or fall, enjoy the ride,
No money exchanged, no profit due,
Though he may give her a buck or two,
Legs entangled, arms entwined,
"Are these yours or are those mine?"
Long French kisses linger on,
Luscious lips, curling tongues,
Romance in an advanced state,
Once teenage stage now adult rate,
Close the curtains, lock all doors,

The missionary position preferred to `all fours`,
Leaping from the wardrobe, swinging from the light,
Singing like Tarzan going ape in the night,
Beating his chest as a dominant gorilla,
A jungle stud intending to thrill her,
She, with large mammeries, glamorous, bare,
Shaking her boobies inducing a stare,
His lips start drooling, oozing saliva,
Seduced by the view of her well-trimmed vagina,
She, in return, is fond of a roast,
His `meat and two veg` stand out the most,
For dessert, a helping of belching cream pie,
Stains on the bed sheets harden when dry.
Bouncing Brenda, no cash or cheques,
Bops up and down simply for sex!

08 February 2020 13:15

Bubble of Love

***

All this instant obsession, this falling in love,
These nonstop sessions, can't get enough,
The constant phone calls that swallow the days,
'You hang up!'...'No! you hang up!'
The verbal interplay,
Those scented flowers delivered,
A card signed with kisses,
Roses for the lady
Who may become his missus,
Perfume sent on Valentines,
No clue who actually sent it
Hoping it's from 'you know who!'
Or else she'll be offended!
A table for two on birthdays
In some fancy restaurant,
Expensive but intended
The event would seal their bond,
He used to jog in mornings
Before they chanced to meet
But now he lies there yawning
With her underneath the sheets,
Dressing gowns at breakfast,
Coffee for caffeine,
He tells her she's the prettiest girl
He has ever seen,
She blushes with the compliment,
Turns to him and smiles,

Takes his hand to reassure
She appreciates his style,
They cuddle, kiss as lovers do,
Cocooned in a bubble of love,
Suited as a perfect pair;
A left- and right-hand glove,
Her photo in his wallet,
His photo in her purse,
Both comforting to glance at
When days can get no worse,
Shifts at work seem endless,
Relentless hours apart,
Suddenly everything seems senseless
In matters of the heart,
Fools rush in, thoughts in a spin,
Where angels fear to tread,
Couples deny the subtlety,
Dive headlong instead,
He who waits hesitates
They say he then gets lost
So, where's the common factor
To decide which bridge to cross?
Obsession is always testing
How strong a bond can be,
It's refreshing to have the blessing
Of a tested destiny,
So, bring on close relationships,
Let all lovers loose,
There're plenty fish out in the sea,
Go catch one if you choose!

28 February 2023 16:59

Bullets and Bombs

***

Bullets and bombs for maximum harm,
Shelling to kill or be killed,
The war ignores fatalities, flaws
Applauds those who fire at free will!

The induction of destruction sets in deep,
Statistics highlight those who've died,
Thousands of casualties wiped off the earth
For reasons no-one can justify!

Heartache, heart-breaking consequence,
Civilians, families torn apart
Either by death, some unfortunate event;
Enlisting seems sadistic from the start!

Mortar bombs, mayhem, delirium,
Utter madness, abolition, the waste,
But when a country attacks you have to fight back
Counteract, retaliate!

Thousands of pounds of ammunition,
Rifles, tanks, missiles,
War doesn't come cheap there's a cost increase
When you add those having lost lives!

It's the same old same old same old thing,
Greed from one person with power

The worst-case scenario, an ego trip
Lengthening by the hour!

Honour the dead with medals, words said
Hold parades, show marks of respect,
While others are falling, we're only just mourning
For young men who futures are wrecked!

Bloodshed on roads and pavements,
Hostile behaviour and threats,
The savagery of the military
The infantry projects!

Destruction, demolition, drastic decisions,
Inquisitions, missions of death,
The squeeze of a trigger ends lives forever
In aid of a governing request!

Bullets and bombs for maximum harm,
Those under threat fire back,
It's a brutal means that leads to extremes;
A combative tit for tat!

07 December 2022 17:01

Canine Conclusion

***

Went for a dog-walk, the air felt fresh,
Buses rushed by, so did the rest,
Rush-hour traffic at its peak,
Hold-ups in the busy streets,
A man on a ladder cleans dirty windows
Concerned with rain not how the wind blows,
Wiping panes with a blade, so slick,
Detergent and water cleared with a flick,
Young mums with prams step in the road,
Walk around the ladder with 'bad luck' moans,
'Nee naw nee naw' ambulance siren,
Cars pull to one side in case someone is dying,
Cyclists continue in cycle lanes
Rumbling, bumping up and down drains,
Shoppers hopping to and fro
Avoiding touching, eyes kept low
For fear of meeting a stranger's gaze
In case they talk what do you say?
Into the park across football fields
Where dogs can charge, let off steam,
No matches today, dogs run free,
Poop-scoops ready... one, two, three,
Joy, delight! the open space,
Watching canines play and chase,
Fun done, leads on, back to paths,
Side-stepping people, locked parked cars,
Over main-streets, zebra crossings,

Back-to-back, packed shoppers shopping,
A short-cut down two alleyways,
Nearly home as daylight fades,
This time of year it gets dark soon
Beckoning the fluorescent moon,
Red-sky setting of redundant sun,
Closure of day as the night's begun,
I sit on the sofa, one thing is odd;
Before my next dog-walk I must get a dog!

10 December 2018 10:29

Celtic Wildlife Gig

***

Declan Dormouse taps his toe
To the fiddler's jaunty tune,
Penny whistle held to lips
Waiting for his cue,
Brogan Bunny strums along
On a battered mandolin,
Worse for wear but who cares
When you hear the song begin?
Seamus Squirrel provides the bass,
A strand of straw in his mouth,
Feeling cool with shades on
(Everything's purple looking out),
Brannon Boar beats the drums,
Body piercings through his snout,
Trotters wielding drumsticks
Giving drums a mighty clout,
Tara Turkey on tambourine,
Steps up to the mike,
Croons some blues; farm chickens
Being cooped up day and night,
At the end, a pause, a ripple of applause
From the paws of animals around,
Shrieks from birds, appreciation
For the quite sensational sound,
The following tune is upbeat,
Up-tempo, unlike the first,
Dancing paws and claws are seen

Shuffling in the dirt,
Brendan Badger (a menagerie mover)
Swaying back and forth,
In his black and white outfit,
Tailor-made of course,
Hannah Hare dances a Bunny Hop
Impressing those who saw
Her effortless, strenuous back-flip
Where she landed on all fours,
Twin sisters, Cahan and Cailin
Break into an Irish jig,
Weasels have flexibility,
Swift agility, are quick,
Several geese line-dancing:
Synchronised webbed-feet,
Goose-stepping in unison
To the band`s outlandish beat,
Woodpeckers swinging in the trees,
Tawny Owls give hoots,
Encouragement for the entertainment
Including the backing group!
Sable, Sachi, Sada,
Melodic, blissfully sweet,
Three harmonious hedgehogs
Make songs sound complete,
The band are pumping, thumping,
Close to finishing their `set`,
Wolf whistles from the wild hounds
(You could never keep as pets),
The noise is almost deafening
As they hit the final note,
Their efforts had faired successfully
Far better than they`d hoped,
Brannon Boar twiddles drumsticks;

A contented happy pig,
As were the animal members
Of the Celtic Wildlife Gig!

Chemotherapy Combat

***

If you break into a smile let me know,
For a while you've been wrestling for an anecdote,
A reason for relief from increasing strain,
The belief that half the man you feel will be whole again,
Meanwhile snuggled in a burrow like some outcast recluse
With eyebrows furrowed; a sign of abuse,
A truce is impossible, no fifty-fifty deal
Nature has a hostile streak with no appeal,
Far from toothless, ruthless, it can subject you to hell,
Put you through paces crazed by cancer cells,
Chemotherapy combat summons a rebellion,
Your system is the victim, explains why you're not well again,
A delicate dilemma void of volunteers
Summoning sympathy from anyone who hears,
The recoil of dread when 'cancer' gets mentioned,
The dropping of heads; an unconscious intention,
The diverting of eyes in order to think,
Overcome the surprise with several blinks,
That struggle to juggle with words to say
When cancers declared, pretence is betrayed,
No turning back, a roller-coaster ride,
Ups and downs, tossed side to side,
Thoughts in a whirl, a cruel descent
Fuelled by the gruelling predicament,
The tablet-habit, popping of pills,
The condition imprisons against the will,
Holds you hostage, secures you in chains,

Denies you freedom you once entertained,
Your liberty is choked, there's a grip on your throat,
A restriction to diction whenever you spoke,
An affliction of pain remains in your chest,
An insane drain on strength you possess,
Where is the logic in who should suffer
This dreaded disease in a hope to recover
From vile vomiting, the indignity
Chemotherapy combat taunts me?

29 April 2023 22:13

Coldest of Dreams

***

Slithers of ice in your coldest of dreams,
The shivers, the shudders, the shakes,
Your mind takes exposure to wild extremes
Imagining cracks as it breaks,
You slip through the surface, water is revealed
Engulfed by the river's depth
Endangered by hypothermia
As the level creeps up to your neck!

Unwilling, spine-chilling thoughts while asleep,
The tremors, dilemmas, the fear,
Falling down mountains capped with snow;
No hold as you fly through the air,
The decline is defined in slow motion,
Frame by frame, one by one,
On the brink of tragedy prolonged agony
You wake with a jolt, feel stunned!

Alone in a snow-filled environment;
Icy depths, upsets, remorse,
Fearing polar bears, blood and violence
The silence does much to endorse,
A heartbeat pounding, nerves jangling,
Your life on a precipice, a cliff,
One slip, delayed moments of dangling

And you're gone in the all-devouring drift!

Perils in subconscious minds at bedtime,
The imaginings, tragedies, the traumas,
The worst-case scenario is where our thinking seems to go,
Maybe an inkling to warn us,
Conclusions drawn caught in snowstorms
Where pillows are crevices of rock
Filled with the latest flurry of flakes
Your nightmare is helpless to stop!

Slithers of ice in your coldest of dreams,
The agony, antagony, the strain,
Your mind overrides the optimistic side
Accepting expected pain,
Dreams are snowed under with danger
Drive you into disarray,
We sleep as rest is a saviour
But dreams lead our minds astray!

Colonel Covid's Memoirs

***

Disillusioned humans suffered,
(We made sure of that),
Took many lives so easily
With mischievous attacks!

You didn't see us coming;
The element of surprise;
Our silent infiltration:
A sensational enterprise!

The mission staged from Wuhan
Enlisting airborne bats;
Our flying assailants
Helped set the deadly trap!

The invasion of numerous countries;
Asian and all the rest
Afraid we'd created
A too-fatal conquest!

We knew we had the advantage,
It's now a well-known fact
Invisible to the naked eye
Humans can't fight back!

Our armies were well positioned
In 'systems' they couldn't refuse,

Especially those undergoing,
Growing health issues!

Our mission proved highly efficient,
Exceeded its expectations,
Bringing friends to a bitter end,
Killing close relations!

Alas! there were serums to fight us,
We had to rapidly retreat,
The enemy understood us more
Than when we were at our peak!

We regrouped, ready for battle,
(Rebel-cells in hiding existed),
Though humans could detect our threat
Outbreaks could not be resisted!

Illness added to our weaponry,
Further strikes laid in wait
But humans had means to intervene,
Minimise their fate!

Confused humans perished,
(We took them by surprise)
But our impact had been shattered;
Attacks neutralised!

Think I'll exit the army,
Become virus-exempt,
A disease-free entity
In my retirement!

07 March 2021 23:02

Colour

***

Discrimination is wearing thin
Over colour of natural skin,
A dark hue is as true
As the person it's in!

Prejudice becomes irrelevant
With the development of time,
Colour of race in second place,
Racism far behind!

Decades of change have rearranged
Attitudes viewed by people,
Taunting of blacks, counteracted,
Outdated, slated, illegal!

Racial abusers are currently losers,
Escape by the skin of their teeth,
Those arrested are constantly questioned
For suggestions they hope to achieve!

Bless those who have suffered,
What's done is done is done,
The indignity is history
Racism overcome!

Discrimination is disappearing
Over colour of natural skin,

Doesn't matter who's black:
As a matter of fact;
The person's important within!

Company Man

***

Company Man
In dungarees,
Standing by his work's machine,
Loyal to his daily routine,
Regular breaks, cups of tea,
Overtime in abundancy,
Extra pay, security,
Income for the family,
Time booked off, hours free,
Two weeks abroad; holiday spree,
Portugal, Spain,
Tenerife, Turkey?
To regenerate
Lost energy,
Revive the decline
With vitamin C
Derived from the sun
Horizontally!

Company Man
Generously paid,
Budgets wisely,
Money saved,
Mortgage in the
Latter stage,
Credit cards
Well arranged,

Settled monthly;
Interest tamed,
Financial stress
Kept at bay,
Red is black,
Debt erased,
No grey areas;
Colourful days!

Company Man
Plays it safe,
Punctual,
Never late,
Arrives on time
Unlike work-mates
Who tease him
On his attendance rates,
Pull his leg,
Say he's two-faced,
Cursing the boss
Then making haste
With an urgent job
To please "his grace"
To stay in favour,
Secure his place
In case redundancy
Dictates!

Company Man,
Squeaky clean,
Unblemished record
Kept pristine,
No half-measures,
No in-between,

One hundred per cent
Perfectly keen,
Years of service,
Daily routine,
Mundane Mondays,
Weekend dreams,
Work contribution
Quite supreme,
Ducking & diving
Controversy,
Rewarded by a
Pension scheme!

Condiments

***

There's a reason for wanting to be seasoned;
Pepper me with love and tender care,
Cover me with layers of attention,
Just a sprinkle, an inkling we can share!

Salt is a compliment to taste buds,
Too much takes a while to overcome
But disregard formalities shake your cellar over me,
Prove to me you're wholly flavoursome!

Salt and pepper are destined to be together,
A natural combination come what may,
Could we follow their tradition, be in the same position
An addition to successful interplay?

A blend of ingredients is often pleasing,
An achievement for companionship acclaim,
If a couple can endeavour to be like salt and pepper
They will stay together; share the same surname!

There's a reason for wanting to be seasoned,
Pepper me with kisses on my cheek,
My love for you is ever increasing,
Condiments are highlights of our week!

18 February 2023 09:16

Consolation Wine

***

Wake up, smell the roses,
Those posing by your bed,
I wanted a lie-in
The boss rang instead,
Work's multiplying;
Electric car sales,
The world needs supplying
Technical details!

When you wake, read my note
It will quickly explain
Work pressure beats leisure
Yet once again,
Please don't be angry
It's scuppered our plans
Work's bread and butter
You must understand!

Today you'll be pacing
One room to another,
Impatiently calling
Your more patient mother,
Complaining remaining
Too often alone,
Work takes priority,
You stay at home!

You cancel the booking,
The restaurant says,
'Thanks for your call
We have other guests!'
You open a bottle
Tip, sip, it tastes fine
A tang on your lips
Of consolation wine!

Sorry I'm busy,
(Reputation on the line),
Sales are essential;
Targets to climb,
Financial expenditure,
Balance to meet,
Increasing temperature,
Feeling the heat!

Wake up, smell the roses
I left by your bed,
I popped to the grocer
Who stocks only red
But those are your favourites
I hope you don't mind
My absence while dabbling
In consolation wine!

06 May 2023 08:02

Contentment and the Ferryman

***

Birds have roosted before darkness,
Embers glow in the evening fire,
The ferry lights extinguished;
The service not for hire,
The boatman goes home famished
After a long day back and forth,
His wife lays food before him;
He's so relieved to be indoors!

He tells her who he met today;
'Pete Ryan and Elmore Green',
A couple suspected of kidnap
Questioned by the constabulary,
Elbows in ribs, shushed whispering,
Gossip in corner shops,
Tittle-tattle behind closed doors
In stores and at bus stops!

"Johnny Bond wants to go fishing,
I told him, "On my next day off!"
"I'll fix our fence before I go
And weed the garden path!"
"Okay!" his wife says fondly
As she kneads fresh dough for a pie,
Her fingers caked in self-raising flour,
Her wedding-ring placed to one side!

Donnie Dougal is proud of his ferry
Having run it for twenty years
Transporting folk to the mainland
From the Irish isle he shares,
Remote and rather desolate,
Residence treasure their privacy,
Outsiders are under suspicion;
Never permitted to feel at ease!

"Ruby love, if you're game enough
We can walk to church on Sunday,
The forecast says the sun will last
We could turn it into a fun day",
Ruby quips, "We can take a trip,
Have a wholesome meal at `The Inn`,
Walk Hanley Bay where the tulips sway
To the strength of the coastal wind!

Another log on the open fire,
Donnie Dougal increases the heat,
Clasps his mug of steaming tea,
Puts up his aching feet,
Ruby settles beside him
Watches `riding` on tv;
Gymkhana events by equestrians
Judged by skill and speed!

Their cottage; warm, comforting:
Thatched roof, flowers, lush lawn;
An idealistic picture
For an artist to have drawn,
The ferry man; a merry man
Contented with his world
A shy Irish so-called lad

With his local Donegal girl!

25 August 2022 12:33

Cosmic Conclusion

***

I recollect with my feet on Earth
When love was light years away
The stars were dull, extinguished
On a dark-side null display!

The planets never aligned themselves,
Too random, too scattered apart,
No cohesion, purpose or reason
Why they should liaise on a chart!

Meteoroids drift in the universe,
Collaboration lost in space,
Patience takes a back-seat
Where chaos is embraced!

Embroiled in continuous lack of light,
Black is the governing mood,
Tracking the path of a satellite
On a radar void of view!

Battered, bruised, this galactic cruise
Leaves erratic trails of gloom,
The feeling's drastic, airborne, static,
The trait of a helium balloon!

Progression in this atmosphere
Is a treacherous journey to take,

No relief, release, lack of sleep
Results in pains and aches!

Any sign of life in this silence?
As strife begins to unfold,
Is there light to follow
From the sorrow, harrowing cold?

Delving in the abyss of all this;
A twist of fortunate fate,
A clearing in the varying sky
Where mist cannot dictate!

I recall it all with my feet on Earth
When love was light years away
But now I thank the heavens above
For your love in a cosmic ray!

12 March 2023 18:27

Curtains

***

Before the cock crows, before night birds rest,
There's delay in the crack of dawn
Portrayed by blackened curtains
In dark clouds not yet drawn,
A single ray of sunlight
Breaks through a weakened spot
Like acetylene flames on metal frames
In a low-lit working shop!

Before the skies surrender
To another day's surprise
Caution goes unattended
Before the curtains rise,
Everyone is vulnerable,
Humbled or elated
Depending on their circumstance
Where fate gets complicated!

Prior to a fresh performance
There's a dormant length of time
Where curtains are left hanging
In suspense where no sun shines;
The blackout of a nighened sky
Which nature has endorsed
Takes centre stage in twilight hours
To silent star applause!

The conventional mist of a morning shift
Hangs in a dawning to come,
A forlorn night retires on a whim,
Expires under rising sun,
Curtains are thrust wide open
Enveloped by the clarity of light,
Hours of hustle and bustle,
Comings and goings of everyday life!

Before the cock crows, before night birds rest
There's a moment of still in the air,
Apprehension peppered with tension
As daylight reappears,
Curtains for the ceremony
Hang between light and dark,
A night and day longevity
Drawn together, pulled apart!

10 June 2023 07:11

Daffodils

***

Flowers in vases on window sills;
The delicate petals of daffodils,
An Easter parade of yellow extreme
Warmed by the sun in an ideal spring scene!

Smiles in bright sunshine, happy domain,
Laughter before any forecast of rain,
Vacant-day holidays beckoning soon
As daffodils bathe in full bloom!

Nectar abundant, pollen for bees,
Nature says 'thank you!' with sincerity,
Manageable charitable acts are key;
Daffodil donation hospitality!

Fresh cut, early bunches at their peak,
'Say it with flowers' and there's no need to speak,
Deep green stems, slim leaves that match,
An endless supply, a constant new batch!

Easter's here, spring has sprung,
Chocolate galore on sweet-toothed tongues,
Confectionery eggs; traditional,
Equal to the sequel of daffodils!

Seas of yellow in fields of green,
An alluring sight, a painter's dream,

Inspiration for a poet's quill;
A flourish of lavish daffodils!

20 March 2023 10:12

Dancing Dougie

***

Dancing Dougie never stops,
Despite being over sixty,
Keeps him fit, his knees don't knock
Though his "ticker" is rather "iffy"!

Standing in the butcher's shop,
Earphones, music on,
His feet begin to shuffle
To an upbeat, tempo song!

First his ankles shudder,
Inspired by twitching toes,
Flinching of his buttocks
In a John Travolta pose!

Pointing to the ceiling
This aged, disco freak
Is so obsessed with 70's dress
He wears it every week!

His earphones are vibrating,
He does a three-sixty twirl,
Shuffles back and forth on legs
That make it all possible!

With a serious expression,
"Dancing like your dad!"

Seems even more hilarious
Next to the butcher's slab!

Physical jerks, throwing shapes,
Counting "one, two, three",
Dancing Dougie struts his stuff,
Holding in false teeth!

His nylon shirt stretches,
It's buttons about to pop,
The collar hanging loosely,
Grey hairs poking out the top!

He seems completely lost in this,
Flicks his tongue at ham,
Flirts with hocks, fresh sausages
As a disco-dancing man!

Break-dancing creates friction,
Spinning round a lot,
This pensioner tries to improvise,
Revolving on his bald-spot!

He grabs a partner, Ethel Reed,
Guides her through a twirl,
Awkward holding a "bag for life"
Crammed with vegetables!

The butcher's queue grows longer,
No-one being served,
No-one complains being entertained
By this disco-dancing nerd!

A flickering tube; his strobe-light,

Risking hernias in his "flares",
Attempts a failed handstand,
Nevertheless, his audience cheers!

Dancing Dougie is a blessing,
Hearing comments people say,
"Shouldn't he be resting?"
Suggesting he acts his age!

A pound of mince, a block of lard,
Dougie leaves the butcher's shop,
Heads for the grocer's, another gig,
Dougie never stops!

Demise

***

Here's to those fallen at such a low cost;
The price of a medal, the expense of a cross,
A dirt-cheap plot with thousands of others:
Sons of sad fathers, offspring of mothers,
Friends in lost battles, foes in war,
Baffled what they're fighting for,
Unparalleled pride with a practised salute
In plush uniform, brushed army boots,
A sense of dignity, new recruit
Interviewed in a three-piece suit,
Hugged, kissed, waved 'goodbye',
Lumps in throats, tears in eyes,
Fears for safety, prayers on lips,
The letting-go of fingertips,
The emptiness, that sense of loss
As window panes lose their frost,
Cold and eerie, bittersweet sad,
The sending-off of a smart, young lad
To support his country, fight the fight,
Risk being caught in enemy's sights,
Kill or be killed, simple tact,
Fire at will while they fire back,
Trading grenades tossed into the fray,
Trained enemy's (not meant to be) last parade,
Death in ditches, wretched scenes
Engraved on the brain, featured in dreams,
Shell-shock flashbacks, nightmare scares,

Waking in sweat, bed sheets share,
Best friends perished, blown to smithereens,
Memories treasured as life used to be,
Flickers of incidents, therapeutic thoughts
Console troubled minds from defining a corpse,
A visit from the military, knock on the door,
"So sorry Mrs. Dismiss, your son's left the war
To be buried with honours, a medal to his name!",
Incredible compliments, moment of fame,
Mother sheds tears, sobs in father's arms,
His attempts to comfort, create a calm,
Peering down from the picture-frame
their one and only son
Smiles for eternity to help them overcome
The heartache for pity's sake, remember him with pride
Taken by some shrapnel in a war of suicide!

15 May 2023 14:11

Diary of a Distant Dormouse

***

Home, where the log fire is burning,
Not alone as the wife dries some spoons
In the massive oak tree named 'Sanctuary'
With ornate, spacious rooms,
Mr Tidmouse sat sunk in a cushion
In an armchair reading his mail
Feeling the heat from a cosy seat
Warming his paws and long tail,
The other armchair is vacant,
It belongs to his faithful Mrs
Who likes to hum her favourite songs
While dusting or washing the dishes,
In the corner a bookcase of hardbacks
'Mouseraker', 'Pawfinger', 'Rodent Royale',
Spy stories are intermingled
Among cook books to simmer and boil,
Framed pictures of many grandchildren
Aligned over the open fire
Account for years that have disappeared
Since they both retired,
Pies in the oven are browning
Mrs Tidmouse bakes some buns
Her blue and white striped dress
Protected by a lemon apron,
She twitches itching whiskers,
Rolls up her cotton sleeves,
Takes care in stirring gravy

While simmering garden peas,
Her husband had been out early
As the pantry was almost bare;
Insects, flowers, berries, seed
And nuts for them to share,
Through ever-so tiny windows
Grows a darkened dismal day,
Wettened soil, mud runs like oil,
Rain on window panes,
Plates full of vegetarian meals
Laid carefully on the table,
A block of wood wedged under one leg
To keep the table stable,
No need for a ticking tick-tock clock
They live wild as indeed did Tarzan
On the mantlepiece looking a treat
A ceramic vase with flowers in,
The peck-pecking of a robin outside the door
Begging with his beak to come inside,
Mr Tidmouse rises to let him in,
A shrill whistle and in he flies,
Shelter from the unwelcomed weather,
Warmth to dry feathers and claws,
Oh! how much better it feels together
The atmosphere indoors,
"Come here!" Mr Tidmouse beckons to his wife,
"Let me hold you, cuddle nice and slow!"
He draws her close, kisses her nose
Under the mistletoe!

20 October 2022 20:52

Edith

***

The rancid aroma of treason
Intermingled with rifle fire
On a cold, callous day
In early morning haze
Where bravery insanely transpires,
Echoes of military footsteps
Indicate seriousness;
A line of assassins
Performing an action
Dictated by a German Fascist!

Dignity hangs in the balance
On a scale of immense magnitude,
Being faced with inevitable "death sentence"
While maintaining a strong attitude,
Principles honoured, adhered to
Require a determined mind,
In the face of self-imposed sacrifice
Derived from aiding mankind!

Uninvited isolation
In a cell of meagre respite,
No sleep or visitation
From salvation overnight,
Moments of meditation,
Periods to pause
Over memories, situations,

No indication of remorse!

A visit from a priest that morning,
October 1915,
A dawn enterprise with watery eyes
Blindfolded as customary
By a German soldier
Aware of the case, his face
Was the last she'd see,
An execution, disillusioning
An irate community!

Eight barrels pointed at her,
Barbaric, inhumane,
A cowardly act, "matter of fact"
Ordeal for military gain,
One bullet to the forehead,
Three buried in her heart,
A post mortem report forwarded
To defy myths from the start!

Her unselfishness stands noted,
She could have stayed at home
In a Norfolk dwelling safer
Than a Belgian danger zone,
But Allies needed saving,
Craving nursing care
Beyond the call of duty
In a ruthless atmosphere!

English Intelligence,
Secrets smuggled through,
The evidence relevant
When her trial was pursued,

Admitting assisting Allies
In their quest to escape
Rubber-stamped a guilty verdict,
Condemned her to her fate!

So honesty's a virtue?
No! not all the while!
Having signed a statement
The day before her trial,
No wearing of nurse's uniform
To pacify the judge
Whose psychic powers claimed "guilty"
Which seemed evidence enough!

Talk of German soldiers "folding"
When told to shoot the nurse,
Nonsensical myths by the media
Served to make it worse,
"The head of the execution
(Maybe an infidel)
Realising she'd feinted
Shot the nurse himself?"

A heroine, a martyr,
Historical claim,
Mentioned with affection,
Edith Cavell by name,
Caring by nature,
Famous worldwide,
Outrage displayed
On the day she died!..
....
Remembered with pride!

Egg Head

***

Easter Bunny stops running,
Doesn't even hop around,
Lost in the woods with a basket of goods,
Wearing a whiskered frown,
Long ears dangling, drooping,
Furry head hung down,
Seated on a tree stump
Emitting a whimpering sound,
His fluffy Bunny tail quivering
Like wasp wings when air bound,
Gnawing on a tight clenched claw
A sharp buck tooth has found,
So a rabbit's foot is lucky?
Though a hare has let him down!

Easter Bunny crying,
Head in wettened paws,
A headstrong hare regretting
Getting lost, going off course,
A diversion through the woodland
Should have saved him extra chores
Of the 'scenic route' which would have suited
Better than remorse
But now he credits the benefits
Of adopting afterthought,
Hindsight means he might have hiked
The long way after all;

The sad case it's a little too late
To remedy this downfall!

Easter Bunny baffled,
Rattled by his mistake,
'If only I'd followed the Yellow Brick Road
Where the Wizard of Oz took place!
Dorothy made the right turn,
This is such a waste,
In a 'rabbit' stew without a clue,
Chocolate egg on my face!'
The sky began to darken
(Such loneliness it creates),
Lots of eerie noises
From which there's no escape,
Bum squeaking time in the tree-lined wild,
Guaranteed to keep you awake!

Easter Bunny bewildered,
Full of frightful fear,
He was used to his bed, not roughing it,
Spending the night out here,
A domesticated rodent
Could get eaten by a bear,
Beaten by some hooligans
Or startled by a deer,
A dark and dismal existence,
A sordid, stark nightmare,
Shivering among the timber,
Wishing to be elsewhere,
Dewdrops hang from nostrils,
A pair of bent Bunny ears!

Easter Bunny bothered,

Unsurprisingly uptight,
Unbelievably blaspheming
In the dark, deprived of sight,
Exaggerated imagination;
Things go bump in the night,
Heart stops, caught on the hop,
His tattered nerves in strife,
Droppings almost everywhere
(Round, choc peanut size),
His rear foot tapping nervously,
Dilated pupils, bloodshot eyes,
Longing for daylight, daybreak,
Morning sun, relief on the rise!

Easter Bunny half awake,
Moreso half asleep,
Tried counting sheep but lost them
(As bad as Little Bo Peep!),
Knackered and distracted
By the lack of any peace,
Wild rabbits looking at him
As a freak among the trees
Carrying a wicker basket
Of chocolate eggs for kiddies,
Something to laugh at,
Taunt and tease,
His size, colour,
Distinct lack of fleas!

Easter Bunny's ears prick up,
An approaching noise fills them,
Excited talking, people walking,
Among them several children,
Christians head this way each year

Carrying a cross as Pilgrims,
`Look mum! the Easter Bunny has come!
To spot him`s a chance in a million!`
He gave them dozens of chocolate eggs.

Enough to easily fill them,
As they led him out from the forest he shouts,
"I'm a happy Bunny! It`s brilliant!"

Everlasting Allies

***

General Concern, Major Catastrophe
Lead their troops into battle,
Several soldiers need the lavatory
Causing delay, more hassle!
"If we reach the trenches this century
I'll be eternally thankful!"
General Concern said, referring to trousers
Hanging down round ankles!

Private Digby, ridiculously
Asked to be excused,
He'd been up all night, blighted
By the effect of plump, stewed prunes,
Fighting a losing battle,
His paunch a blown balloon,
Finely primed, ignited,
Likely to go "boom",
Ready to explode like
Hand grenades do!

Major Catastrophe, drinking tea
When the enemy attacked,
Throwing bricks and stones
He ordered privates to throw back,
His army was quite barmy,
Nowhere near Iraq,
A bunch of part-time

Amateurs in fact!

Butchers, bakers, candlestick-makers,
Almost every available trade
Made to wear the uniform,
Turn out in grand parades
From ragged houses in baggy trousers
Carrying guns and blades,
Pretending to be soldiers,
Bold and brave!

Halfway there they turned around
Due to lack of ammunition,
Norman the storeman left a note,
"Rod and I gone fishing!"
With nothing to fire
They had less desire
To face the fiery opposition!

Four soldiers had dental appointments,
Excuses to stay behind,
A tooth or two (though untrue)
Needed seeing to, you'll find,
Army life proved stressful,
As with teeth it was such a grind,
"Why do dentists look down in the mouth?
You think they'd cheer up sometimes!"

General Concern had a telegram
In the form of a "Dear John" letter,
His wife ran off with an athlete
Who'd received a coward's white-feather,
He knew he was "in for the high jump";
The bar too high to endeavour,

He would have joined the army
But he never!

Out came the sun; "currant bun",
The soldiers felt relaxed,
Decided to sunbathe
Instead of making tracks,
Rows of tanning torsos
Stretched out in underpants,
Ignoring the drone
Of enemy tanks!

Soon they were surrounded,
Surrendered and serene,
The Kapitan made a motion,
A tailgate lowered, two cases revealed
A supply of suntan lotion,
It turned out the Russians
Were even less keen
To have a war discussion!

Board games were favourite,
"Throw a six to start!"
Draughts, snakes and ladders, portable bingo,
The Russians were at war but had a good laugh
As the English tried to understand their lingo,
"Bobby Charlton!" the only English you could distinguish,
That plus, "John, Paul, George and Ringo!"

General Concern, Major Catastrophe
Gave up on the war,
Played soccer, downed vodka
Ending up on all fours,
Liaised with the Russians,

Behaved like juveniles,
Enemies; a non-entity:
Everlasting allies!

***

Family Outing

***

Fundraising raffles at the annual scout fete,
Countless rows of stalls on parade,
Darts thrown at playing cards with careful aim,
Amusements designed to entertain!

Toffee apples, candy floss, hot dogs for sale,
An aroma of onions as a jazz band plays,
For the young, Punch and Judy, a painted-on face,
One soap and water can erase!

Fairground rides, a miniature carousel,
Drench-A-Wench, Guess the Stench of a home concocted smell,
Test your strength, swing the hammer at length, attempt to ring the bell,
Crustaceans sold at seafood stalls; winkles in their shells!

A beer tent for the thirsty, strictly over eighteens,
A marquee selling hot chips and slushy, mushy peas,
A screaming child had lost her mother temporarily,
She's reunited much to her relief!

Helium-balloons on a string, multi-flavoured ice cream,
Displays of fine confectionery (coconut toffee),
Children play excitedly, psyched up with energy,
Adults sipping teas and warming coffee!

Black clouds overhead represent a major threat,

Everyone's aware of a rumbling sound,
Everybody's hoping they don't get a soaking
Heading for the exit homeward bound!

03 August 2020 10:49

Farmyard Comedian

***

Ma 'n' Pa's best friends have come to stay
For a break, a holiday, few days away
From the hustle, bustle of city stress
In favour of country, rural rest,
Jean, Cecil, sweet LeeAnne Lou,
That gem of a girl from private school,
They stayed last time for two whole weeks,
LeeAnne is grand, has a fine physique,
Fifteen years of feminine bliss
(I wonder what she's like to kiss?),
I'm fourteen; at that curious age
Where the need to impress is at centre stage,
We live with animals, Ma 'n' Pa have a farm,
Sheep out to graze, cows in the barn,
I could show LeeAnne a thing or two,
Demonstrate my aptitude,
I lead her to the chicken run,
Juggle eggs but drop some,
I walk along the pig-pen rail,
Arms outstretched so as not to fail,
One foot slips, in I flop
Among the mud and the thick pig's slop!
LeeAnne laughs, it wasn't my aim,
Covered in pig shit, smelling of drains,
After a clean-up I show her the horses,
Nostrils flare, she stops and pauses,
I stroke their noses to keep them calm

But Elsie the filly nips my arm,
LeeAnne chuckles amused by my face;
An embarrassed grimace (horse-teeth shaped),
I've got to impress her, win her over
With manly gestures, brave manoeuvres,
Riding bareback must do the trick,
Phillip the stallion is bigger than big,
I throw myself upon his back,
"Giddy up Phillip! let's make tracks!"
Gravity is cynical, leaves me numb,
A rodeo victim holding his bum!
LeeAnne shrieks with utter joy,
"You really are a comical boy!"
I feel the anguish, there's no pretence,
A fallen equestrian with no horse sense,
We take to the fields where the dipped sheep graze,
The new-born lambs frolic and play,
Gambol happily, delightful to watch
When suddenly there's a hoof in my crotch,
Doubling up, excruciating pain,
A sheepish grin from LeeAnne again,
There's a shallow river, no bridge to cross,
Only stepping stones if you don't slip off,
Surely, it's my time to shine,
Leave predicaments far behind,
Gain some credit, impress this girl
Who I must confess dresses well,
Avoiding the water, three quarters way there,
A knee-deep, boot-seeping, wet-sock affair!
LeeAnne laughs, tears rolling down cheeks,
Foundation she's wearing has several streaks,
The cows come to greet us as if to chat,
Doris, Stephanie, Agnes, cow Pat,
We sit on the fence as the milk-cattle 'moo',

Overbalanced I land in a pile of wet poo!
Reeking, stinking, red-faced, irate,
Even hit in the face standing on a lost rake,
She'll never be in awe of me, dishevelled, soaked,
Seeing me sadly as a constant joke,
LeeAnne Lou, well amused, can't wait to tell her friends
About the Farmyard Comedian she
stayed with last weekend!

Figure Of Eight

***

You're circling my mind in a figure of eight,
A non-stop circuit, no pit-stop break,
Speeding on corners, slowing on the straights,
It should be the other way round, I'm afraid!
But you, a non-conformist, a rebel since your teens
Will revel in the devilry of non-conformity,
A sure-shot competitor aiming for first place,
Just room on the rostrum for your posturing face,
I see the champagne bottle already in your hands,
Popping the cork with only one thought 'you are in command',
If someone should overtake, forsake you on the track,
A campaign of hate would escalate, there'd be no turning back,
Take the bends with uncertainty, dodge what lies ahead,
Weave in and out of difficulties as if these give street-cred,
I'm watching from the main stand, your bland expression; stressed,
Hidden under a helmet, visibility is less,
If I don't see you passing I confidently wait,
Relying on the design of the figure of eight,
It triggers my mind into thinking of you
Driving at speed in all that you do,
Brakes are cosmetic when desperate to inject
A white-knuckle ride that hits you direct,
The shudder, vibrations shaking your frame
Provide the sensations you crave time again,
Fire in your belly, desire to be best,
You're rigged to a hot wire of shock distress,

Going for the jugular, not varicose veins,
They're reserved for drivers in the slow lane,
Your speedometer registers 'one hundred and ten',
Two wheels on the track contemplating bends,
Lapping 'strays' delayed way behind,
The sort who resort to biding their time,
Happy to drift in nonchalant ways,
To simply exist, fulfil their day,
But that isn't you, you're revving your engine
At the front of the queue with ambitious intention,
Making a statement, breaking new grounds,
Expressing yourself, standing out from the crowd,
Original thoughts that make me debate
Why I'm thinking of you in your figure of eight,
Going round and round a monotonous circuit,
A carbuncled tyre; the worst is to burst it,
You can be let down, upset now and then,
Deflated, upstaged by so-called friends,
Some say 'put you first' but they put you last,
Even the lapped car will eventually pass,
So you leave them standing, abandoned by the road
If they show signs of antagonising moods,
You have drive, passion, crashing is taboo,
Interaction is fashionable with 'funky dudes',
Oddball people feature in your life,
Left-of-centre is one way they're described,
This is my cue, my claim to fame,
Topping your list is my very own name,
Watching you socialise, circulate
With your circle of friends in a figure of eight!

Finger Licks and Card Tricks

***

Magic is mesmerising, mystical,
Those who believe have a plan
To convert the non-conformist
With a cunning sleight of hand!

The conjurer leans towards devious
In mischievous words and moves,
They tantalise and tease us
With seamless points to prove!

Finger licks and card tricks,
You pick the Ace of Spades,
It disappears before your eyes
Despite a constant gaze!

Eggshells pulled from nowhere,
The occasional dove or two,
You're working out the method
But you haven't got a clue!

Top hats are quite 'old hat',
White rabbits never feature,
Magic in the modern sphere
Rarely features creatures!

Sealed boxes with your name inside,
No sign of a magic wand,

The modern-day illusionist
Is there one day......then gone!

02 June 2023 23:07

Flight of the Helium Balloon

***

Helium balloon drifting away,
The child's head a speck from where it came,
The trees a cluster of green-shaded leaves,
The minority rustic from winter's siege,
They dance periodically caught by the wind,
Crazily swaying in unison,
Small farmyard animals, miniature cows,
Miniature villages, minuscule towns,
Lots of fields, flocks of sheep;
Cotton wool in several heaps,
Wheat-filled haystacks, Weetabix mounds,
Home-grown breakfast standing around,
Birds like flies flitting below
Resemble insects, even the crows,
Whirls of smoke from chimney tops,
Curl like cigarette swirls non-stop,
Is that a tractor, the reddish blur,
Or a farmer-driven harvester?
It's awkward to tell, hard to decipher
So high in the sky, no binoculars either,
Rivers run riot among the land,
Inked in blue, some grey and bland,
Country roads, rural, unmarked,
Plunged in blackness after dark,
Follow their routes, many sharp bends,
No signposts, certain roads come to dead ends,
Trees; cauliflower, broccoli branches,

The mind plays tricks when you're guessing the answers,
What's that down there, can't make it out?
After climbing so high we're flying through clouds,
Temperature drop, less pressure, less wind,
A melancholy, folly drifting,
Way above earth, far from the ties,
Tourniquets tighten, blood pressures rise,
A blissful floating, light on the air,
No sound destination, going nowhere,
An inflated hobo, hardly discreet,
Bright red in colour, entirely unique.
Helium balloon slowly on the descent,
It's power, it's glory eventually spent,
Losing its altitude, fuelled by gas,
Cruising down gently in a silent crash,
Resting unattended in a meadow of dew,
Inquisitive insects, an animal or two,
There is a label attached to its knot,
It says, 'Friends Forever Are Never Forgot!'

24 February 2019 14:26

Frostie the Doughman

***

Cold on the corner
Of a freezing, cold night,
Temperatures nearing the
Scale of frostbite,
Hibernating fingers linger in gloves,
The tingle of warmth in a winter so rough,
Visible breathing seen in the air,
Projected jets of steam appear,
A single figure under a tree
Half hidden; disclosed partially,
Trainers with protruding tongue,
Baseball cap, sunglasses on,
Of dark persuasion; Nigerian:
A dreadlocked Rastafarian,
It's ten o'clock, a distinctive sound;
Trodden ice on snowy ground,
A quick exchange, a plastic bag,
A roll of notes in elastic band,
Off he goes, our figure waits
Approached by others who hesitate,
Look for signs that implement the Law,
Photographs taken from neighbouring doors,
A group of officers strategically placed
Ready to swoop, give offenders a chase,
These are possibilities involved in the war
Between the police, those trying to 'score',
Drug dealers plying their trade while they can,

Supplying these dudes, 'How d'you do? hey man!'
Hastened business in case of trouble,
Hanging around only makes trouble double,
Money is massive, the dealer knows and
That's why he's nicknamed Frostie the Doughman!
Dealing in weather it's better to avoid,
Freezing his balls till his sperm's paranoid,
Counting his money, riding his luck,
Massing a fortune of unlawful bucks,
Prepared to shake, condemned to shiver,
Fend off the cold to 'stand and deliver'
As a highwayman accumulating riches
'But they get 'a hit' the fucking bitches!'
His 'heavies' visit those in debt,
Bloody noses, arms round necks,
Promises of payments soon,
Ailments have delayed debts due,
Excuses wane, impatience tenses,
'Pay or there'll be consequences!'
Punters left in sorry heaps
Prodded, punched right off their feet,
Reminded to be more forthcoming,
'Your days are numbered, the Grim Reaper's humming!'
'Jeepers creepers! where do we turn?
Our drug addiction has us ruined!
There's no reprieve, no respite,
We need 'speed' in our heads tonight!'
Topsy turvy predicament, sick of being trapped,
Knuckles rapped by steroid bullies,
their intimidating six-packs,
In a jam for certain, all fire-doors are closed,
Aid is not forthcoming, everyone is indisposed,
Jail terms for possession and distribution I am told
Of class A drugs is tradition if convictions tend to hold

But it's Christmas let the business raise spirits
This festive season
Then Frostie the Doughman can be arrested
For good reason!

Girlfriend

***

I loved you lovely Lolita
Like a panting dog on heat
Trouble is when we kissed
I smelled your cheesy feet!

That day I held your hand
On the sand when I felt bolder
The waves crashed in, I guess the wind
Disguised your body odour!

We'd walk, the sun would wear us down
We had to stop and sit,
The heat was overwhelming
As were your sweaty armpits!

I was never one to raise my voice
Make a noise, 'kick up a stink'
I never complained, mentioned your name
But you really did 'pen and ink!'

We sang, we danced, had a teenage romance,
Held each other in a clench,
I admit though I'd blow my nose
If only to stifle the stench!

I'd buy roses for your birthday,
You said you loved their scent

But never questioned your present of
A case of deodorant!

Some people have no sense of smell,
Bad breath is often strong,
Others turn their head aside
To ostracize the pong!

Sometimes it's embarrassing
When people walk away,
With itching, twitching nostrils
And a look of stunned dismay!

While visiting a wildlife park
The hay was neatly bundled,
No-one was immune from your rancid fumes
Even the pigs were disgruntled!

I loved you lovely Lolita
Wherever you are, I wish you well,
Guess you're married to a laddie
Who has no sense of smell!

24 February 2023 18:37

Glass Ballerina

***

Glass ballerina pirouettes
To The Dance of The Sugar Plum Fairy,
Reflected in the mirror of the jewellery box;
A routine that never varies!

Trinkets, rings and bracelets,
Pearl necklaces lay within,
Trays, Aladdin's Cave to the girl
Intrigued as the ballerina spins!

Her mum stands in the kitchen
Rolling pastry for a pie,
The girl in mother's bedroom
Has a curiosity pry!

She tries the clip-on earrings,
Admires them in the mirror,
Checks a beaded necklace
As mother prepares dinner!

Rings too large for fingers
On the ten-year-old young girl,
She slides them on regardless
Infatuated by the jewels!

She discovers two old brooches
Grandmother used to wear,

Now of sentimental value
To validate passed years!

There's make-up on the dressing-table,
Lipstick on her lips,
Foundation smeared across her face,
Mascara on fingertips!

She grooms her hair with mother's brush,
Dabs blusher on her cheeks,
Eyeliner on her lashes;
Far too heavy: unsteady streaks!

Mother calls her daughter,
"Dinner's ready, wash your hands!"
She laughs to see her youngster
With the coloured face she'd 'crayoned'!

"I'll teach you make-up later!" she says
As the girl arrives,
Sets plates upon the table
With a casserole piled high!

Glass ballerina pirouettes
To The Dance of The Sugar Plum Fairy,
Reflected in the mirror of the jewellery box;
A routine that never varies!

02 March 2021 20:27

Granite

***

Can you find it in yourself to love somebody else
Or are you still content on your own?
You're solid as rock withstanding hard knocks
As independent as a single stone!

Are you happy at ease doing as you please'
A freelance female on the loose?
Wise to any ties of the romantic kind,
Coming and going as you choose!

Have you given thought you might be caught
In a somewhat close relationship by chance?
An unorthodox method which leaves you tethered
To a male with irresistible advance!

Everyone needs someone at sometime
But full-time is too big a call
A gamble you're certainly not prepared to take
In case it hits a brick wall!

More questions than answers, mysteries to solve,
You prefer it plain and simple on your own,
No tangles or rivals, risk of being stifled
By a list of trivialities on your phone!

Will you ever see yourself loving somebody else
Either new or a person you have known?

You're solid as rock withstanding hard knocks
As independent as a single stone!

26 October 2022 19:24

Hallelujah

***

I hear hallelujahs are free,
Boy! I'm gonna get me some,
Put Jesus on a pedestal
So he's ever still number one!
Read the hardback Bible,
'Maze at all the tales
Of his struggles, constant troubles
In biblionic detail,
I claim a hallelujah!
It's written in the stars,
I punch the sky with a clenched fist,
A victorious shout of, "Rarr!"
My faith is given a 'kick-start',
The engine's in first gear,
Can I claim a hallelujah
If I kneel and say a prayer?
I've gone to several churches
Seen the light through stained glass windows,
The font, the pews, the clergyman's loo,
I've resisted innuendos,
I say 'grace' before I eat a meal,
'Pardon me' if I burp,
I've developed a taste for Jesus Christ
My freezer will preserve,
Do I hear a hallelujah?
Good lord! yes I do,
Even though I say it myself

It sounds too good to be true,
When a youngster I was Christened
Although I had no choice,
While growing up I wrestled
With questions, paranoid,
Where is this godly figure
When you need him the most?
No email address in times of stress,
Can't even leave a note,
I light candles, wear brown sandals,
Sometimes a long, white gown
But fear impersonation
Will bring my status down,
God, this drives me crazy
When I ask to repent my sins,
A little voice inside my head
Says, "Where do I begin?"
I sing hymns from memory
With every good intent,
'Onward Christian Soldiers'
Though I never knew where they went,
Knocking on people's doors I implore,
"Have you found Jesus?"
They tell me they've got things to do,
"We'll let you know if he sees us!"
I've joined a 'happy clappy' band,
Acoustic guitars and song,
We make-out in the market square,
Get shoppers to sing along,
'Jesus Christ Our Saviour
Sales save us being drained,
Praise the Lord we can afford
A McDonald's with the change'!
I pray for Daphne Dildo

And her grandfather clock,
Convinced he was the one and only
Relation she had got,
Her mind; on another planet,
She speaks to neighbours and friends,
Claims she's been watching Dallas
With several aliens,
I help support the homeless,
Volunteer to dish out soup,
Don't ask what particular flavour
As it's reminiscent of puke!
I help distribute Christmas cards
For charities and fetes,
Starting early in August
So as not to leave it late,
It deserves a hallelujah!
Sock it to you kind of shout,
I'm claiming this is mainly
What my aim is all about!

Hay Lay

***

Ambient atmosphere,
Crisp, crackled hay
Baking in sunshine
Beneath where I lay,
Bird song in unison
Oscillating around,
A shrill, tantalising,
Energising sound,
Wood pigeons flutter
In foliage of trees,
The process of mating
Creating babies,
Bumble-bees buzzing,
Wildflower friends,
The gathering of pollen
Borrowed from stamens,
The intricate insight
To insects unfurls
As you delve uninvited
Into their world
Of shortened lifespan,
Food for birds
Worms and grubs,
Hunger cured,
Dragonflies visiting
Rivers and streams,
Hovering suspended,

Mosquito feed,
Midges, moths,
Butterflies too
Are part of their diet
On their quiet daily cruise,
Beware of those frogs
With a strong appetite
Who devour dragonflies
Should they lower in flight,
Nature's resources
Takes all in her stride,
Survival denial
Provides other life,
The daily melee
Of feast or die,
Flourish encouragement,
Multiply,
The wily kingfisher
Has cunning and tact
To catch swimming
Minnows and sticklebacks,
Swift and skilful,
Elongated beaks
Perfect to trap fish,
Tasty treats,
The occasional rabbit
Sits up and waits,
Ears detect danger
To wager escape,
Scampering bobtails,
Fur on the run
Disturbs other animals
Unnerved, overcome,
The rustle of leaves,

Swishing of tails,
All diving for cover
With outstretched nails,
Camouflaged 'mirage'
Blending with leaves,
Simulating bark
On age-old trees,
Nature's a bonnie lass,
Full of intrigue,
Intricate, an instant hit
With life's ideology.
Relaxed atmosphere,
Brittle, dry hay,
A comfortable cushion
Beneath where I lay,
Birds warbling solos,
A cacophony of noise,
I would stay through the day
If I had the choice!

12 February 2023 11:09

Her Majesty's Pleasure Deterrent

***

The jangling of metal, keys turning in locks,
Security measures on the prison block,
Cell-doors banging, echoes through halls,
Only wardens moving in corridors,
Prisoners segregated, lock-down complete,
Inmates sedated, kept off the streets,
Jaded, isolated, serving their term,
Their penance; jail sentence, to reform and learn,
Hours of boredom locked in one cell
Playing card games with hard names of prison clientele,
Chess for the studious, noughts and crosses for some,
Privileges for the privileged, various scams are run,
Gangs, intimidation, schemes to achieve drugs,
The worst kept secrets are widespread enough,
Internal dealings, tit-for-tat,
A bar of soap for a toothpaste cap,
Toilet rolls exchanged for crisps,
(Prawn cocktail flavour, hard to resist),
New recruits, come on in! here's your prison number,
No referring to your first name,
It's your surname you'll come under,
Bend over in the strip search as far as you can,
Your anal region may conceal illegal contraband,
If you're a daily smoker, take your smoker's kit,
A sample of tobacco, a lighter to get lit,
Change into your prison clothes,
Part of your welcome pack,

Join the team of residents whose outfits are exact,
Step in, sit down, look around, this is the 'Induction ring',
Your introduction to prison life whatever strife it brings,
You already knew wardens are 'screws'
But that's not disrespect,
It's a name they gained;
'Keys turning in locks' which have a similar effect,
'Early birds' are volunteers for mornings in the gym,
Wardens call if you want to exercise your right to be slim,
Breakfast is at seven; cornflakes, jam on toast,
There's half an hour to devour, no time to get engrossed,
Chosen occupations resume at eight o'clock,
Three hours of self-creation, education for good stock,
Back on 'the wing' at eleven, dinner is at twelve,
The majority say it's poor quality;
The taste indistinguishable,
One o'clock back at 'work', concentration until five,
Socialising until eight; pool tables, games apply,
Danger during 'yard' walks, inmates intermingle,
Attacks in showers, unsupervised hours,
Outcomes are unthinkable,
Attention on the 'nonces' who've sexually offended,
Targeted by inmates if they find them unattended,
Apprehended on a separate 'wing',
A precaution assignment,
A surety for security; solitary confinement,
Children in bewilderment, 'where has father gone?'
Concocted stories offered to distraught daughters and sons,
When older they are told the truth as it's too much to bear
At such an influential age to undergo despair,
Recordings can be made on disc by fathers locked away;
Stories read personally or messages to convey,
Siblings can hear his voice, it helps to keep in touch,
They naturally have the choice, it matters oh so much,

Her Majesty's Pleasure deterrent holds
A measure of attraction,
Prisoners released can't cope on the street,
Performing criminal action,
Breaking their curfews, arrested on purpose,
Reintroduced back again
To the comfort, the perks;
Hot meals, clean shirts, the routine every day,
A life of retribution usually resolved in prison
Is not drab for all prisoners; if you think it's bad, it isn't!

22 December 2018 16:33

Hokey Cokey Voting

***

Let's all vote in the Referendum,
Seal envelopes,
Post and send them,
A cross in the box
'Remain' or 'Go'
At the Polling Station,
Rain or snow,
Rooms at schools
Commandeered for the day,
Pubs and clubs
Host the Polling cabaret,
Rolling up in numbers
Having stayed up late
Studying blips and blunders,
Both sides of the debate!
Eighteen years upwards,
The legal age to vote,
Pioneering, sharing
A future full of hope,
Bonuses for voting 'in',
The onus is on 'out',
Hokey Cokey Voting,
Shake it all about,
Differences of opinion,
Drastic points of view,
Divisions in decisions
Over what to say and do,

Matters concerning issues,
Discussions deal with points,
Conclusions deluded
If you haven't made a choice,
The act of pen to paper
In a square declares your aim,
Denotes which choice you favour,
Undecided you abstain,
Secrecy is an option,
No compulsion to reveal
Where you place your cross
In the ballot box
Performed in secrecy,
No misleading cheating,
Precautions held throughout,
Classed as a crime if you falsify
A vote for someone else,
No looking over shoulders,
Officials follow rules,
Don't give them doubt to cast you out
Or vote you overruled,
Savour your big moment,
Milk it, take your time,
Flex your muscles powerfully,
Jerk your head from side to side,
Come on like a Gladiator,
The arena is all yours,
You're in control of the pen you hold,
Wield it like a sword,
Everyone has their moment,
Their claim, one minute of fame,
Don't write it off, draw your cross,
The crowds will chant your name,
Let's all support the Referendum,

Every entry counts,
With Hokey Cokey Voting
You can shake it all about!

Hospital Patience

***

The nurse had a deadpan expression,
Her patient, a bedpan obsession,
Attempts at its removal
Were met with disapproval,
When it's too full objections might lessen!

Patients constantly pestering,
Nurses never objecting,
They enjoy what they do
But give them their dues
They could use a booster injection!

The patient had trouble undressing,
Baring his body was stressing,
You have to laugh
When he had a bed-bath
He wrapped his thing in a dressing!

Hospital wards were cram-packed,
Beds wedged in back-to-back,
Patients walked around
In hospital gowns
Revealing their arses and crack!

Patients were often awkward,
Not backward in coming forward,
Pestering nurses

(Under breath curses),
Swear words in effing all wards!

Doctors are seldom jocular,
As distant as long-range binoculars,
They do their job well
But you can never tell
If you're favoured or unpopular!

Operations are quite a sensation,
Take a while for recuperation,
There are gurgles and squeaks
From patients asleep
Recovering from sedation!

Walking wounded in A and E,
Groans, broken bones, agony,
Anxious for treatment,
Someone to relieve them
From "ohs!", "ouches!" and "eees!"

Doctors and nurses
Provide a good service,
Demand is bursting at the seams,
Trolleys in corridors,
Hospitals crammed wall to wall;
An increase in their popularity!

Appointments for consultation
Mean one or two hours waiting,
Studying the ceiling,
Uneasy feeling,
Avoiding the stranger you're facing!

If you can't take a bus
It's too much fuss
Playing "spot the parking space!"
Shunting bumpers
Of cars in front of us
To win the parking race!

Aches, pains, sores,
Confusing corridors,
Reception gives directions if you ask,
People wandering in a maze
Wondering why it takes all day,
Finding where to go is such a task!

Ambulances outside,
Instant access denied,
An understaffed, overworked dilemma,
Patients breathing one last breath
Often a matter of life or death
Depending on a technicality error!

Road barred, placards,
One-day strike by irate staff,
Traditional in this modern day and age,
Unfair hours, sub-standard pay,
Chanting, shouting, having their say,
Protesting in a most persuasive way!

Twenty-four hours, night and day,
Hospitals function come what may,
Sometimes taken for granted by us all,
The medical service never sleeps,
A wake-up call emergency,
Let's put our hands together and applaud!

Irish Incident

***

When Irish eyes are smiling
Why are yours so sad?
Is it loneliness on this island,
The isolation, the habitat?
The chit-chat of locals,
Scandal and strife
Exchanged on street corners
In order to excite?

The cottage we live in
Is minimal, quite bare,
Limited in comfort,
Far from debonair,
The cow's milk we tender,
Sell to the shop
Is essential income;
Worth every drop!

The Sabbath day church bells
Ring rather slow
Bring the primitive villagers
Together in tow,
The reverend O'Brian
Conducts 'confession',
Issues 'Hail Marys'
With every blessed session!

One public house,
No jukebox installed,
Just fiddlers with bows
Playing tunes they recall,
Traditional folk songs,
Acapella style,
Solos sung so low;
Inaudible for a while!

Red-sun horizons
On landscapes of beauty,
Irish sea tosses and turns
Continuity,
Boats sailing out
On a fishermen's quest,
Tattoos of anchors
Inked on their chest!

Rum, vodka,
Tobacco and smoke,
Natural temptations
To partake, unprovoked,
Wine, whisky,
A slick Irish jig
On the soil of an island
Not spoiled by oil rigs!

We're sister and brother,
Earn coins where we can,
Hot stews from a pot;
Nourishing: grand,
Your tongue has a temper
Which leaves me 'floored'
With objections to why

I let 'donkey' indoors!

Police here are criminal,
Sinners of crime,
No diligence, innocence,
Victims of bribes,
The Garda is rather
A haven of sorts
For underhand deals,
Maverick courts!

You told me quite coldly
You're leaving the Isle,
Life is so lowly
You're glad there's no child,
Besides, my habits
Are hard to maintain,
"I find that damn donkey
Indoors once again!"

Goodbye dear sister
Can't resist one last hug,
I already miss you
(An issue with love),
You fade in the distance
Embraced by the sea,
I stand mesmerised
Watching waves from the quay!

Two months on you're still gone
But a letter arrived,
"Come over to live,
There's a bed, better life!"
"Sorry dear sis

I've decided to stay!
This Isle is my home
Where my heart remains!"

When Irish eyes were smiling
Why were yours so sad?
No romance in your daily plans
Or love life to be had,
I understand your logic,
This existence left you bored,
With losses there are perks and gains;
The donkey's back indoors!

15 March 2023 20:02

Jolly Folly

***

Why do rabbits have the habit,
Stand in country roads
Risking to be squished by tyres,
Suicidal bucks and does?
'Rabbits caught in headlights'
Is how the saying goes,
I wish they'd eat the grass in fields,
Not dodge cars like toads!

Why do snails never fail
To spread across wet paths
With pedestrians destined
To break their shells in half,
Not intentionally, accidentally
Their mentality is in doubt,
Why risk being homeless
With no payments on your house?

Why do worms wriggle and squirm
Across damp paving slabs
At the mercy of dirty
Boots with tread that traps
Mud and stones, anything prone
Lying on the ground,
Why risk being a fatalist
The early bird hasn't found?

Eager rooks and seagulls
Lurking in the road,
Flapping wings, fighting
Over scraps of fallen food,
Never mind the traffic
With beaks crammed with buns,
Screeching brakes, close escapes
From being overrun!

Cats and squirrels act like fools;
Chase across the streets,
Seem to wait, hesitate
For vehicle increase,
Perhaps they love the challenge
Darting in and out of wheels,
But they should tread more carefully
Or feel how real tread feels!

06 May 2023 19:37

Junkie Astronaut

***

She's high in a sky of planetary illusions,
Earth looms somewhere down below,
She's piecing together a puzzle of confusion,
Disillusions she longs to disown,
Lightweight, floating, constantly hoping
This trip will help her sustain
A source of control, mental hold
Instead of `cold turkey` disdain!

She's flying, applying herself in mid air
Appearing to others around
To be endeared by a narcotic snare
Elevated by powder well ground,
Inhaled by snorts through nostrils
Flared for maximum effect,
A risk to the nose, lethal overdose;
A possible hospital prospect!

She's encountering mazes of irrational thought,
Those that craze, derange minds,
Hallucinations of provocation
To chill any unwilling spine,
Bizarre situations in random locations,
A euphoria of unexplained fate,
Wild adventures that conjure tension,
Apprehension to contemplate!

She's in an orbit of consistent revolution,
An intrusion to the meteors and stars,
An unwelcome inclusion to the institution;
An overcrowded universe by far,
Her welfare is launched on a cocaine base
Which hastens the countdown with speed,
All systems go as time escalates
Her mind into fantasy!

She follows the sun on its journey through space
Lost in a haze of magnitude,
Her drug addiction causing friction
Overseen by the light of the moon,
During her 'fix' she's out there
On a high, on a cloud, in flight,
No fixed address in her loneliness,
No destiny; out of sight!

She wallows in home-made self-pity,
Thinks the world is a treacherous place,
Wants to escape at the ready
Whenever temptation dictates,
She loves to float in drug daydreams
With the aid of narcotics she's bought
She aims to fly high as a name transpires;
She's a junkie astronaut!

19 November 2022 12:16

King and Queen Festival

***

Bless the court jester he's nobody's 'fool',
Entertains guests with success as a rule,
Dressed in bright tights, a bell on each foot,
A multi-coloured outfit to enhance his look,
Juggles with balls suspended in air,
Receives the applause, the encores, the cheers,
Tells medieval jokes, some obscene,
The crowd laughs after the king and queen,
Songs to savour; a ditty or two:
Singalongs for the motley crew,
The Castle of Aragon is happy and gay,
Flagons of ale on bales of hay,
Full-bosomed wenches perched on laps
Arms round necks of inebriated chaps,
There's dancing, prancing in Olde English style,
Heavy, thick wigs, 'gentlemen' smiles,
Minstrels' harmonies, tunes on a lute,
The recorder, Vielle (violin substitute),
A hogshead on the table, carvings of pig,
Roasts of beef; magnifique!
The drone of loud voices, conversations unheard
Drown by the volume of inaudible words,
High antics, high spirits, sky-high party mood,
Gallons to drink, a banquet of food,
Guards on duty missing the fun
Armed with crossbows to kill or stun,
Defend the castle in case of attack,

Deny any enemies; defy their impact,
Death by sword, slain by blade,
A bloody, ruthless escapade,
Hot tar on assailants scaling walls
Catapults, slings, sharp swishing swords,
Defence is relentless, survival a 'must'
Among rivals a liable degree of mistrust,
Armies of loyalty royally bound
To one king and queen; the Sovereign Crown.

Bless the court jester for light entertainment
Distracting people from troubles and ailments,
Performing tricks, the 'sleight of hand',
Quick wit and jokes somewhat pre-planned,
Revelling in the party mood
Adding joy to the wine, the food,
A relief from hardships; temporary reprieve:
A rare, shared opportunity
To 'push the boat out', let off steam
In an evening fit for a king and queen,
Laughter, dancing, jollities,
A rare invite for a social scene,
Music played on a mandolin;
Nimble picking of fickle strings,
Kissing, cuddling, canoodling couples
Cavorting with contagious chuckles,
Delirious shrieks from women folk
Paired with medieval blokes,
Encouraged by the wine intake
A 'straight to the head' intoxicate-state
But still, it flows from primitive casks
No limit imposed, no questions asked,
Drink to the limit of no return
From the hangover blues and a morning ruined

Through amorous antics, frivolous fun
Worth more than a gold medallion,
Liberty, freedom, release from stress;
Reeling from the feeling of happiness,
Party capers, a real-time experience
Having attended you rate your appearance,
Beyond this occasion so many drawbacks;
Increasing diseases, enemy attacks,
For just one evening relax the rules
Bring on the acts; the court jester: the 'fool'
Let all the people enjoy themselves
With their king and queen festival!

12 August 2022 13:35

Lather In Love

***

There's lather in love
If massaged enough,
It can shine with lustrous appeal
Or disposition to a dull condition
Bottled-up, vacuum sealed!

An ingredient in caring
Blended with sharing
Produces a heart-warming glow,
The combination brings expectation
But no complacency though!

Watered-down contempt
Weakens offence,
Dilution is the solution it's evident,
As difficulties dissolve, problems resolved,
Disposed of, discarded as sediment!

Chalk and cheese
Make a 'no-go' recipe,
They don't agree even from the start,
Square pegs in round holes have a similar role
On the whole try to keep them apart!

Any love and tenderness
Is perfect, endless,
It's senseless to ever deny,

Even those who're penniless can afford to lend this,
It's worth more than money can buy!

Peace and harmony
Is the ultimate key
But too short-lived; outrun,
There's always a negative influence,
Some incident to overcome!

There's lather in love,
Lots of bubbles and stuff
Coupled with a soap-sud feel,
Don't keep it hid, flip off the lid,
Don't let the contents congeal.

25 November 2022 22:40

Lucifer

***

The devil inside, face red and wild
With fiery hottened breath,
A contorted expression of anger
In a wrangle of total unrest!

A skin of crimson texture
Scorched as a Mexican sky,
Burning as molten larva
Sliding down a mountainside!

Bloodshot eyes with white exterior
That pierce with fearful cold,
Frightening fangs, a tongue which hangs
Salivating for your soul!

Long nails for mass destruction,
Any obstruction in its path
To tear, maim, claw eyes to drain
Blood in the aftermath!

A tail of some proportion
Strong as a leathered whip,
Lashes scarring flesh
Would make the hardiest submit!

Patterns across its body
Show an attitude of hate,

Scorn, complete resentment
Vent at the human race!

Its horns project sheer terror;
An epitome of kill,
Weapons that could gorge with force
Remorseless at freewill!

With cloven hooves this tyrant,
A trident in its hand,
Violence in its nature,
Hateful devilish plans!

Seeped in hostile tyranny,
Cruelty beyond repair
The devil detests chivalry
Invests in endless fear!

Face red and wild, the devil inside
Anticipates confrontation,
Lethal fangs, hunger pangs
For the angst it will be tasting!

Lucifer (as Christians prefer),
A name overheard while debating,
A typical fable, the rebellion of angels;
Named with the trademark of Satan!

14 March 2023 21:57

Malice of The Deer Hunter

***

Swift is the arrow which pierced her heart,
Took her down in a whimper of pain,
The buckling of knees, the delicacy
Of death in a frozen frame!

No warning of what was about to come,
An orphaned fawn standing alone,
Reflected in eyes; a mother who dies
In a life-changing perilous zone!

The hunter smirks satisfaction,
Approaches the unfortunate prey,
She catches a glimpse of her youngster
As the dwindling life in her fades!

The fawn disappears out of instinct
Thrust into a world of threats,
Away from the herd, alone, disturbed,
One step from a nervous wreck!

Vulnerable, inconsolable,
Deprived of her guardian-mum
She wanders in hope to finally regroup
With the herd she had come from!

Days of endless searching,
Nights spent anxiously

Watching every movement
For homely company!

At last, she spies some antlers
In the distance; home at last!
Her searching has paid dividends
As she shares delicious grass!

Malice of the deer hunter
Void of guilt or shame
Sports an inflated ego
To emphasise his name!

20 April 2023 10:22

Maritime Myth

***

Her lips were hot from kissing the sun,
They glistened with Vaseline,
She spoke very little as to where she was from
Even less as to where she had been,
Her tan was Mediterranean,
Her eyes a deep ocean blue,
A scaled, marine body at the tail end
Where human legs would protrude!

Her wrists were aching from caressing the stars
Which filtered between her fingers,
Thousands of gleams; solar powered
Burning bright with a light that lingers,
Neptune's very own grandchild;
A female with sea-faring features
A maritime myth in the ocean adrift
Among other mysterious creatures!

She's a silhouette betrayed by a full moon's glare
Appearing on the static water's calm,
Baubles of sea salt sliding down her back
Colliding in a stack along her arms,
A swish of her tail in a frenzy
Causes disturbing mini waves,
She turns in spirals of seduction
Thrusts her bosom on display!

She dances with the whale, the porpoise
In a graceful, gracious choreography,
Dipping in the swimming, swirling ocean
On a coastline lined with coral reefs,
There's freedom in a water's depth to wallow,
Liberation to be found in a current's flow,
A world of underwater undiscovered
Thwarted by deep density below!

Marine fish tend to follow where she travels,
Worshipped as a famed celebrity,
All kinds of species with aquatic greetings
Swimming beside her playfully,
She's a maritime myth often kissed
By seals as they roll in fast waves,
The hiss of white surf when her body's immersed
As she flicks the fins of her tail!

23 May 2022 14:29

O.T.T

***

Whatever appeals to you, whatever applies,
Whatever the outcome I cannot deny
You go in guns blazing, dive in head first,
Deny consequences though you might come off worse,
In for a penny in for a pound,
Despite inflation your bet is sound,
No resisting a risk, take the bull by the horns,
Pieces on chessboards sacrifice pawns;
You'll lose now and then but gain in the main,
Maximum effort in the fast lane,
The finishing tape is never far off,
You'll be first to break it, have the last laugh,
Your insatiable appetite for life as it is
Living on the edge of a steep precipice,
Never looking down, never looking back,
Forever on the path of an unexplored track,
Pumped with excitement, hyped for thrills,
Delighted with mystery intrigue fulfils,
The strange unknown of growing concern,
An ingest of interest makes you yearn,
Stern, spurned chances lead to regret
But you have the answer to always expect
A means to advance, a sequence of luck,
Frequent achievements however abrupt,
A slice of good fortune here and there,
Right people to talk to, opinions to share,
You're one go-getter, getting what's going,

What you don't know isn't worth knowing,
You're at the top, a dizzy height,
Vertigo is out of sight,
You've time for lovers, for others in need
Of general guidance, your expertise,
Advice on matters that happen to arise,
Come out of the blue in unusual disguise,
Your uplifting approach, befitting charm
Induces the victim with addictive calm,
A natural gift from the day you were born,
A consoling aura; cosy, warm,
Toasty, woozy benevolent balm,
An elegant welcome with open arms,
A bragger of adjectives, unabashed praise
The heat at the top of any hot flames,
The sparkle in gems, their remarkable gleam,
The startled reaction whenever seen,
A sensation, revelation, braced for fun,
Ready to race when the day is done,
Stretching my mind to exceptional extreme,
Over the top extremities!

14 April 2023 10:56

Penny For the Guy

***

Just steps from the street where people sleep
In doorways where they are laid
Huddled to retain the heat
In woollens plucked and frayed!

Expressions born of restlessness
Etched upon their faces
A trail of hard-luck stories
In too many callous cases!

Cups for coins of sympathy
Dropped by passers-by,
A penny for their private thoughts,
A penny for the guy!

Homelessness is loneliness,
Estranged by next of kin
On the low ebb of society
When the tide comes rushing in!

Blankets strewn on concrete,
Haven taken in shop doors,
Some glances wreak of prejudice at those
Cross-legged on the floor!

We hear a repetitious voice;
The Big Issue sold nearby,

Most dismiss a copy
But the vendor has to try!

Low-life in the high streets,
An increase through the years,
Individuals suffer insolvency;
Caught in financial snares!

Pennies for your kind support,
A penny for the guy,
A little goes a long way
In the homeless enterprise!

29 September 2022 15:30

Plastic Love

***

Plastic love is brittle and thin,
Has little substance from within,
Breaks too easily as pressure increases,
Shatters, collapses in fragments and pieces!

Plastic love is artificial,
Second-rate, never official,
A mere substitute for the real thing,
A fake mistake, second string!

Plastic love is imitation;
A souvenir, a consolation,
A medallion of silver or bronze
As gold is favoured well beyond!

Plastic love feels harsh to touch,
Is insincere, insecure as such,
Is easily scratched, bashed and dented,
Too fragile to be complimented!

Real love is kosher, genuine, bliss,
Blue-sky horizons, alive, sun-kissed,
A boon to the system, home and dry,
Lovers insisting they're satisfied!

14 May 2023 20:12

Psychic Sandman

***

Sandman, mythical handy man
In your dungarees, steel-capped boots,
Hard-hat for health and safety
The nineteenth century introduced!

Your services are voluntary,
Never a profitable scheme,
Millions of children have been fulfilled
By your magical ethos of dreams!

Strict rules and regulations,
No graduation or doctor's degree,
Myths don't age or need changing,
Generations have always believed!

Sandman, has a plan and
Performs it professionally,
When sleep is deprived, he induces the eyes
To a state of tranquillity!

A sprinkle of mystical sleep-dust
Over eyelids half awake,
Mumblings in some foreign tongue
The Sandman undertakes!

No human sees the Sandman,
Sightings are void and vary,

Myths, however, socialise whenever;
'High fives!' with the silent Tooth Fairy!

Excited boys in pyjamas,
Girls in pink night dresses
Far too high on exuberance
Taking nuisance to excesses!

Enter the psychic Sandman,
A bag thrown over his arm,
The age of the child is irrelevant,
They revel in his charm!

Counting sheep doesn't guarantee sleep
Even those who are heavy sleepers,
A child might worry if shy-sheep scurried,
Ran off......the little bleaters!

Hooray! to the brave psychic Sandman
Risking all for young brothers and sisters,
He works round the clock, his deeds are non-stop
Exceeds those of Father Christmas!

11 March 2023 09:19

Pursuit of Positivity

***

Credit to the passionate;
Those who give their all
While others find it fashionable
To act incapable,
Effort is praiseworthy
In any task or test,
Opportunities are there to seize
Or the task is meaningless!

Five stars for enthusiasm
Spurring others on;
An example to those lacking
Back-tracking what has gone,
The need for motivation
Some creation that inspires
A level of achievement
To raise the bar higher!

Praise to all inventors
Thinking 'out of the box',
Defying convention
With the unorthodox,
Progressive thinking,
Alternative ideas,
A boost for morale
To bolster careers!

A nod to the optimists
Adopting 'glass half full',
'Best foot forward!' say chiropodists,
'Anything is possible!'
Positivity going forward,
Negativity looking back,
With hope there's opportunity,
Scope to stay on track!

Say 'yes' to progression
As stalemate is so drab
Change could reveal the destiny
You thought you never had,
Chance is a widening estuary
Which leads to deeper depths,
An ocean to explore the core
Of what you might expect!

Merit to the hopeful kind
Who find sublime success
Not having succumbed to falling behind;
Settle for second best,
Thumbs up for the activists
Whose campaigns mean the most,
Elected through the catalyst
Of maximum votes!

05 August 2022 14:03

Rainbow Dream

***

A treasure of love for beginners,
Those who are willing to learn
How affection finds a direction
To the heart of those concerned!

Somewhere over the rainbow
Where whispered wishes come true,
Technicolour dreams of how it could be
If only for a fortunate few!

Embraces of physicality,
Indications of `holding on`,
Visuals of individuals
In clinches prolonged!

Vows of devotion, dedication,
One and one-only intent,
Promises of love in an ocean
Where plenty more fish frequent!

Long live the life-long tradition,
The kissing of lips and cheeks,
The crucial, therapeutic beauty
Far from obsolete!

Across the expanse of relationships
With their ups, their predictable downs,

Successes and reckless failures
For which they are renowned!

Under the radar... a saviour,
Love on a pedestal,
Available as a pick n mix;
Choose your partner well!

A casket of gems for beginners,
Those resigned, inclined to stay keen,
Nurture the love they're thinking of,
Follow that rainbow dream!

26 April 2023 07:36

Ruby and my Rabbit

***

You remind me of my rabbit
With your sticky-up ears,
Your buck-toothed teeth,
Googley stares,
The way you gnaw carrots
After they've peeled,
Raw, sautéed,
Boiled or steamed,
You're partial to vegetables,
That's no surprise,
You've no cauliflower ears
But beetroot red eyes,
You stomp your foot
When nothing suits
As does my rabbit
With attitude,
Nibbling straw like a country hick
While you gnaw
Potato sticks,
Lettuce leaves are
Crisp, crunchy,
My rabbit sits
Contentedly munching,
You both love salad,
I mean no offence
But what a bizarre
Coincidence!

She's a doe
And you're a girl,
Pure white teeth
Like oyster pearls,
She has the knack
To sometimes hide,
A little on the
Nervous side,
An outstretched hand,
A stroke on the neck
Is my technique
To good effect,
It soothes the soul,
Cools the blood,
Human or rodent
Or cows chewing cud,
The bond is ruined
Without a degree
Of touch upon paws,
The left or right knee,
A rub of the nose
When faces are close,
A scraping of claws,
The chafing of toes,
That intimate moment
As birds beak to beak,
The absurd connection;
Cheek to cheek!
I adore you Ruby;
Your animal habits,
You well and truly are
Just like my rabbit!

27 February 2023 11:34

Sandlewood Secondary Modern School and the Comic Strip Gate-Crasher

***

Ben Bogus scribbles on his desk
(Dirty nails, scruffily dressed),
Grubby shorts, a hanging-out vest,
A bruise on his knee
From a tree conquest!

Sarah Sooch, behind him in class
Listens to teacher teaching art,
Ben, using a penknife carves a heart;
His name and Sarah's in the centre part!

Wally Wimp sings in the school choir,
They nip his bum, his voice gets higher,
Tom Toot lets down teachers' tyres,
When accused he says they're bias!

Ballsie passes wind in Maths,
Divides fresh air, multiplies foul gas,
Subtracts smiles with his flatulence act,
It all adds up when air is trapped!

Sheila Wheeler, a devout bookworm
Reads love stories, makes boys squirm,
Their reputations would face ruin
Being seen with a girl reading Mills and Boon!

Pamela Pigmy teases the lads,
Has small breasts, wears bra pads,
Kisses the boys in the chemistry lab,
Some coy, some enjoy being sex mad!

Hearts under desk lids, drawn on walls
In discreet letters, millimetres tall,
`Lilly loves Clifford` though she also loves Paul,
Her taste for the boys is insatiable!

Hilary Hump is almost in tears,
She`s forgotten her lunchbox first time this year,
Gordon Glip offers her crisps, ginger beer,
She`s a Cheese and Onion munching, burping girl
In school wear gear!

Patrick Pond wears sideburns long,
Ankle-swingers ironed by his mum,
Off to school, `Got your handkerchief son?
Other children call him `mummy`s boy`
Poking schoolboy fun!

Valerie Vole likes school, is always alert,
First to put her hand up, finish her homework,
Maisie Mo wears necklines low, hoists up her skirt,
Known as the `school bicycle`; classroom flirt!

Jeremy Johnson seems overweight,
Never leaves any food on his dinner plate,
Exercise encourages complaints,
His flubber judders round his rubbery waist!

Poor ol` sore ol` Naomi Looth,
Caught by a hockey stick, loses a tooth,

Now the wind blows in, in a direct route,
She whistles while playing her flute!

Dorothy Dunk has a rebellious streak,
Illegal tattoos on both bum cheeks,
A pair of eagles with enormous beaks
Inked by a gink in a back street!

Reggie Press is strange I suppose,
Crams coloured wax crayons up his nose,
Obstructed nostrils! rushed to hospital
To have the blockages removed!

Michelle Ludd wears a pink pullover,
Smells of hamster-bedding odour,
Smells a rat when classed `a loner`,
Other children back off; disown her!

Martin Moron thinks he`s hard,
Looks for scraps in the full schoolyard,
Empties satchels, provokes and snarls,
Anger Management is probable!

Dennis the menace! what`s he doing here?
He belongs in the Beano (has done for years),
A comic-strip character gate-crashing this poem,
It`s best to conclude, leave well alone!

Serenity

***

Sitting there, long hair,
Bushy beard, quiet,
`Under the influence`
Though he'd probably deny it,
A whimsical mood, hassle-free, relaxed,
Mesmerized by reggae;
Bob Marley tracks,
White skin, dreadlocks,
A Rastafarian image,
Influenced by the affluence
Of Africans he mimics,
Incense in a burner,
An aromatic smell,
Jasmine fills the room
Creates a mood spiritual,
Repetition of the back beat
Nullifies the brain,
Dope stupefies energy rise,
The combination drains,
Weed, `grass` it's all a laugh
Unless it leads to `acid`,
Heavy drugs are `lethal bugs`,
Uncontrolled they cause a hazard,
By the by an innocent `high`,
Gentle guitar picking,
He strums long notes, his head afloat
As reefer smoke is thickening,

'Cool man!' he says drooling,
Two fingers raised for Peace,
If only it were true man
World troubles would decrease!
A flash-back to the sixties,
Optimism standing proud,
The submissive Permissive Society;
Illegal indulgence allowed,
Going 'on a trip' had new meaning,
It wasn't by car or plane
But a self-induced substance
With hallucinatory gain,
Cannabis should be made legal,
Some say it ought to be banned
Claiming it messes with people,
Leaves them feeble, weak and bland,
Debate is there for discussion,
Nothing will alter views,
Whichever side you favour
You've an open mind to choose,
Narcotics are optional,
A percentage think they're gross,
Those who over indulge are prone
To take an overdose,
Fine in moderation,
Intake under control,
Mistaken use of habitual drugs
When addiction's taken hold!
Sitting there, no apparent care,
Comfortably resigned,
Humming tunes familiar
Recorded in their prime,
Psychedelic images,
Heavy 'underground' bands

Performing in the seventies
To Afghan coated fans,
Long songs, self-indulgent,
Drum solos rolling on,
Guitar-breaks till your head aches
As it would exposed to sun,
Music of the selective type
Not aimed at any chart,
Commercialism was frowned upon
As it lacked a 'genuine heart',
Song-writing troubadours
Renowned for penning lyrics,
Worshipped by their followers,
Criticised by cynics,
Skinheads loved their reggae,
West Indian, Jamaican style,
Wore 'Bovver' boots and braces,
Classed leather jackets vile,
Mods and Rockers clashes
Televised on the coast,
Opposed beliefs and fashions
Each other believed in most,
The eighties saw a disco age
Relegating rock and roll,
The dance scene, slick routines
Demonstrating foot control,
Punk fans, Indie bands,
A nineties institution
Protesting against convention
With a back-to-roots revolution,
Modern music mayhem,
Expletives by the score,
Once considered an outrage,
Permitted even more,

Effing this, effing that,
Effing till we yawn,
It's a sin new generation's
Consider it the 'norm'!
Sitting there, no-one near,
Unhindered, undisturbed,
Untroubled undeniably;
Happy in his world!

Sixties Child

***

Multi-coloured mayhem
In the eyes of a `sixties` child,
Carnaby Street proved fashionable
In rash outlandish style,
Outfits with military drill,
Frills on a feminine blouse
Worn by males of various age
As a statement in the crowds!

The age of experimentation,
Hallucinations, LSD,
Pot, cocaine, 'acid' brains
Deranged in ecstasy,
'Hip' 'cool' trendsetters
Wearing feathers, the odd kaftan,
Smoking joints in Afghan coats
Repeatedly saying 'man'!

Ridicule from elders;
Parents much more wise
Witness this delinquent sequence
Madly materialise,
Flower Power found its roots with shoots,
Blossomed overnight,
'Wake up and smell the roses man!
Cosmic! out of sight!'

Talk of revolutions rising
Demoralising peace,
Paralysing campaigns relying
On conflict decrease,
Solutions led by dreamers
Seen as fantasy freaks
Wearing rose-tinted glasses
In the face of defeat!

Festival music;
Psychedelic stuff,
Bare chests painted
With symbols of love,
Wild, sporadic dancing,
Promiscuous acts,
Jig-a-jig permissive 'chicks'
Flat on their backs!

Whiskers, beards,
The thinking-man's attire,
Long hair unisex-wear
Geared to inspire,
Heavy 'tracks' on vinyl,
Long solos on drums,
Self-indulgence abundant
While chewing chewing-gum!

'Can't get enough free-love,
Live and let live,
If you can't love your lover
Love who you're with,
Release those restrictions,
Freedom of speech,
Demonstration liberation,

Practise what you preach'!

The rich smell of incense
Infiltrated from rooms,
Musk had an odour
Of proven perfume,
Tarot card readers
Told fortunes to come
Hung heavy with breathy
Opium!

Fond memories how it used to be
In the heart of a `sixties` child,
Sober post-war solemnity
In jeopardy; out of style,
Fun for the young incessantly
Going gung-ho, going wild,
A fresh approach condemning
The `nifty fifties` after its trial!

28 October 2020 22:48

Smokin` Roy and the Bad Boys

***

"I've come for ma boy!" snarled Smokin` Roy,
A six-shooter in his hand,
Backed by a drove of uncouth rogues
To emphasize the plan,
Sheriff Stone was startled,
Struggled to his feet
(It's a nasty surprise opening your eyes
To these guys straight from sleep!)

"Don't do anything hasty!"
Warned Sheriff Stone, eyeing his gun,
"Just show me the keys to set ma boy free,
He's ma one and only son!"
Despite opposition Sheriff Stone propositioned,
"He` got to stand trial for his crimes,
A dozen chickens went missing,
That's a lot of chicken-pie!"

"I ain't foolin`!" Smokin` Roy drooled,
"Do you want lead in your gut?
Hand over ma son or else we'll have fun
Kickin` your sore-ass butt!"
Sheriff Stone relented, a gun to his temple,
Unlocked the strong jail door,
They roped him to his chair,
Secured a neckerchief to his jaw!

Smokin` Roy's son Billy
Came out "whooping" on a high,
Punched the air in cowboy flares
They wear in Illinois,
An arm around his father,
Laughing as they left,
"You'll pay for this!"
Growled Sheriff Stone,
"So far it's free!" Roy said!

Deputy Dennis found the sheriff
Struggling in the chair,
Ungagged, untied the binds,
"What's been happening here?"
"Billy Bone's been busted out
By Smokin` Roy and his gang!
Quick! get a posse together,
You know where they all hang!"

Deputy Dennis rounded them up,
Sozzled Sid was drunk,
Kept sliding sideways off his horse,
Facing back to front,
"Follow me!" cried Sheriff Stone
Galloping to the West,
Feeling a breeze around his knees
While tucking in his vest!

They discovered a trail of horse hooves
From town across the prairie,
Followed the route in hot pursuit,
Sweat-soaked and hairy,
Stetsons protect from sunlight,
The glare of which is strong,

It's imperative that the sheriff's
Not kept in the shade too long!

They smell a charcoal bonfire,
Crawl behind large rocks,
There's Smokin' Roy and the Bad Boys
Drying sweaty socks,
Dulcid Don plays a guitar
Singing campfire songs,
Accompanied by farting
And an alarming baked-bean pong!

Sheriff Stone gave the word,
Took them by surprise,
Dupe released their horses
So they couldn't run and ride,
"What the fuck!" screamed Frankie,
Spitting tobacco phlegm,
"We've been rumbled!" Arnie grumbled
As the posse bundled in!

A confused, muddled struggle,
Fisticuffs galore,
A scorching of bums, flames too strong
From the campfire as it roared,
Smokin' Roy and the Bad Boys
Were overcome, too tired
After drinking Western Whisky;
Not a shot was fired!

Tongue-tied, hands tied,
The gang were forced to walk
The whole way back to Tawny Town
Now they had been caught,

Their horses loose, unsaddled,
Innocent, free of crime,
Loved their new found liberty,
Went completely wild!

Back in the sheriff's office,
Jail door open wide,
The gang crammed in like a sardine tin,
Standing side by side,
"I need a pee!" said Willy McGee
Recovering his breath,
Sheriff Stone remained unmoved,
"There's a bucket to your left!"

Squashed up tight, all night,
Jail not big enough,
Sleep takes over, heads on shoulders,
Piles of cowboy dandruff,
Mud-stained jeans, wet dreams,
Can-Can Saloon girls' drawers,
Dreaming of actually being
Well-hung like a horse!

In the morning the jury sworn in
Before the early trial,
Smokin' Roy and the Bad Boys
Chained together when they arrive,
"You've been accused of abduction,
Corrupting Law and Order!"
Accused Judge Fudge holding a grudge
Against low rankers, those poorer!

Sheriff Stone explained in full
Events that lead to the trial,

How he was outnumbered
And succumbed to feeling riled,
A relentless Judge Fudge sentenced
The whole gang to be shot,
Due to a mild Alzheimer's
He forgot!

"What are these people doing here?"
He asked the courtroom twice,
"They're being tried!" someone cried,
"Really! is that right?"
Judge Fudge, hard of hearing said,
"You say they're seeming tired!
I think it's best they get some rest
Let's end this tiring trial!"

What a farce it all had been,
Unpunished crimes in the West,
An incompetent judge you couldn't trust
With a children's IQ test,
Law and Order in disorder
In a state, in Illinois,
Reputation deprivation of
Smokin' Roy and the Bad Boys!

Soul-Singer

***

Cd cover shows another
Of your poses for the public,
Looking moody, somewhat broody,
Just the way they love it!
A smooth chin with dimples in,
Thick black, gelled-back hair,
A piercing in your eyebrow
To express a modern flair,
A deep tan from some foreign land
Where the sun sets late each day
To impress fans while planning
A tour that scans the whole UK,
A Bolton born Northerner,
A backing-singer long ago,
Deciding to take a risky break;
Pride in going solo,
A gamble but you managed
To make it a success,
Promote your name
Fame came almost effortless,
Soul was your genre,
A single in the charts,
A Top Ten hit for the market
Which appealed to broken hearts,
An increase in venues,
Restaurant menus more familiar,
A beneficiary of popularity

As they often didn't bill you,
Female admirers sighing,
Crying as you sing
Of love lost in relationships
That tears at frail heartstrings,
Gatherings at stage-doors,
Recognition in receptions,
You became a household name
Through genuine affection,
Your manager handles you
With a contract firm and fair,
Financial stability
In your singing career,
The ability to connect
Affects the minds of those
Who listen with attentiveness
To your high notes and the lows,
Taking emotions
To unknown extremes,
Touching on seduction,
Disruptive hard-luck themes,
Your debut album settles
In the number one spot,
Pound loads of downloads,
Sales in umpteen shops,
Personal appearances
To promote sales even more,
Songs sung acoustically
In jam-packed music stores,
Delivered as they used to be
While busking in shop doors,
A guitar case for loose change
Left open on the pavement,
Cover versions rendered

Offered different arrangements,
These brought the breakthrough
That made you a star,
Uncovered, discovered
Your voice and guitar,
Gave you a contact,
It all seemed surreal,
Signing contracts
Your act was sealed,
Up-tempo bookings,
A single on sale,
Vainly good looking,
A stack of fan mail,
Links to females
You've not even met,
Papers' mistakes
Are unfortunate,
They interview those
Who've known you for years,
Dig out the gremlins,
Scandals and fears
Hoping the public-eye
Cries real tears
With revelations, sensations,
Denials, affairs!
All that's part and parcel
Where fame is included,
Privacy invaded,
Life intruded
But there again
You probably knew it!
Anonymous days
Well and truly gone,
You've made it,

Come right through,
Your undeniable talent
Underlined,
Defined,
Approved!

Spanish Flair

***

Place a lucky penny in the young girl's palm
Her dance is a joy to behold
With captivating twists and turns
At only ten years old!

The street is lined with shoppers
Who stop to watch and smile,
Her father plays Flamenco tunes,
Mentors her dance style!

Both of Spanish origin
Egged-on by the crowd,
The entertainment is encouraging,
The appreciation loud!

Castanets are evident,
Relevant to the beat,
Her fingers snap, she clicks and clacks
While stomping agile feet!

Coins are dropped into a case,
Bystanders give her tips,
She thanks them with a knowing nod,
Swivels supple hips!

Rows of mobile phones held high
Recording video clips,

Playback no delay, in fact,
Interacted by fingertips!

The weather often varies,
'Who cares!' the show goes on,
Our ten-year old out in the cold
Although the wind is strong!

Father asks concerningly
If she'd rather stop,
She laughs and says discerningly,
'Not now I'm warmed up pop!'

Flamenco dancing in the market
Induces Spanish flair,
An unusual sight for shopper's delight,
A novelty to share!

Press a lucky penny in the young girl's palm,
Her dance is a joy to witness,
On the 24th, the eve, backed by garlands and wreaths
Guarantee a Merry Christmas!

04 December 2022 21:41

Spider Rant

***

"Why don't they look where they're going?
Lift up their lowered heads,
They'd avoid the irritating crazing of
Walking into cobwebs,
Hours of constant labour,
I've been up since early dawn,
Weaving designs of various kinds
To bind a web, now torn!
How would the humans like it
If I could wreck their home,
Wait for completion of housework
Before trashing every room?
Turn over chairs and tables,
Shatter drinking glasses,
Scrawl graffiti on the walls,
Urinate on carpets,
Have exciting pillow fights,
Feathers in the air,
Bash each other round the skull,
Laughing as we cheer,
Lighting outdoor fireworks
On the oven hob,
Rockets hit the ceiling,
Bangers bang a lot!
Red wine soaks the three-piece,
Difficult to remove,
Vomit gushed upon it

Would be sick to stomach so
Let's tip beer over the hi-fi,
High-five as we go,
Wreck the joint to prove a point
In a spiteful 'heave ho!',
Show no regrets for upsets,
Smash plates in the sink,
Make mockery of the crockery,
Cutlery extinct,
Vandalise the garden shed,
Throw out all the tools,
When used additional cobwebs break,
Makes us feel abused,
In the winter warmth indoors
Substitutes lack of heat,
Our haven on the ceiling
Is destroyed in one foul sweep,
Humans are destructible,
Inconsiderate 'beings',
Anti arachnid antagonists
(If you get my meaning),
Declaring war if we're in the bath
Having climbed the water pipe,
Trying to flush us down the drain
Is ever so impolite,
We never wear bathing costumes,
We're naked as nature intended,
No trunks or revealing bikinis
Needed, no-one is offended,
Why oh why is there screaming
From certain irrational types,
We're just spiders minding our business
On a wall in the house day or night?
Panic stricken, delirious,

On the verge of a heart attack,
Will we be spared by someone who cares
Or given a fatal whack?
Eight spindly legs seem disturbing,
The way we scurry about,
Crawl into cracks during suspect attacks,
Reluctant to venture out,
Let's dance the Spider Quick Step
As we start the carpet chase,
Size nine shoes trying to ruin
The contours of my face,
Leave me deadened, truly embedded
On the tread of a dreaded sole
For having the audacity
To enter inhabited homes!
Why don't they look where they're going,
Raise their eyes to see what's ahead?
There'd be no fussing, no cussing about
Walking into cobwebs,
Hours of dedication,
An artistic work of art,
Disregarded instantly,
Simply torn apart!"

Spite of the Night Dreamweaver

***

Dreamweaver, thought-deceiver,
Leans on pillows at night,
Awaiting sleep to dig in deep,
Ransack your personal insight!

Dreamweaver, misbeliever,
Black eyes dark as coal,
Scheming whatever you're dreaming,
Adopting the dominant role!

Dreamweaver, nightmare-retriever,
Creepier if seen in moonlight,
Motionless as it focuses
On an opportune moment to strike!

Dreamweaver, never keener
Than when you're comatose,
All alone on your own
In a semi-twilight doze!

Dreamweaver, midnight-griever,
A wry smile on its lips,
Closed eyelids are the sign that gives
It license to take grip!

Dreamweaver, bad-breath breather
Seeps into your brain,

Leaks poisoned thoughts, boils and warts
That nightmares seem to claim!

Dreamweaver, blood-fest bleeder
Colours, gleams bright red,
Horrific x-certificate
Unprohibited scenes of dread!

Dreamweaver, hot-sweat fever,
Wet foreheads, mopping brows,
Dreamweaver has an evil streak
That shouldn't be allowed!

04 May 2023 22:53

Sugar Rush

***

You're my cherry bake-well baby,
I'm your slice of apple pie,
Love the crazy things you say to me,
'Bramley! fruity guy!'
I have a duty to defend you
Even when we are apart,
There's a jealous pie that tends to
Tell her friends that you're a tart!
She's got flaky, pasty pastry
Verging on her 'best before',
Says things rather hastily
As skin sheds to the floor,
That sausage roll called Ronnie
Always seen with tomato sauce,
Ketchup lipstick on his cheeks
From the bottle-neck where it pours,
Don't interfere, it's their affair,
Voluntary, not a duty,
Some things go together;
Ronnie Roll and his red-faced cutey!

You're my cherry bake-well baby,
I'm your slice of apple pie,
I know you want to praise me,
Say I'm tasty all the while,
I love your juicy cherries,
Your shaped well, baked-well tin,

So does Brian Blackberry,
I'm not racist over him
But he chases all the females,
Nips their pips, grips bits and moans,
He wants to make you merry,
Squeeze your cherries to the stone,
I know you're not promiscuous,
Not that kind of girl,
Should I trust you with your busty crust,
Burned and slightly curled?
You're a dish there's no denying,
Wish I had a piece of you,
You could be my sugar rush
And I could be yours too!

Swagger Fly

***

Bubba Bluebottle, swagger fly,
Throwin' da shapes wid da moosic on high,
Baseball cap on back to front,
A shufflin', hustlin' publicity stunt,
Google eyes revolving, giant-size wings,
Like helicopter blades rapidly whizzing,
Break-dancing on the chopping board,
Escaping knives as bread is sawed,
Impressive moves, never collides,
Such an extrovert swagger fly,
A refuse attitude rubbish-tip freak,
The stench of forgotten, rotten stale meat,
He reeks, stinks as a drunk with alcohol,
An odour of a repulsive, convulsive aerosol,
Stalking open dustbins, walking over fruit,
Has a fungi fetish for fowl smelling juice,
Putrid green egg flan, bacteria leery cheese,
Burnt fried sausages dripping in grease,
Tomato sauce smeared down recycle bins
Surrounded by flies, `Come on, tuck in!`
The troop of pesky parasites converging on waste
Have an undesirable, vile sense of taste,
Take your eye off foodstuff they land in a sec,
Nuzzle your ice-cream until you detect
You're sharing dessert, its being hijacked
By a gate-crashing pest you want to squash flat,
A swish of the hand and off it goes

Or so you think but you never know,
Yes! It's back, it likes the cherry flavour,
The feel of its feet on the oyster-shell wafer,
It's called for backup, here come the others,
Additional flies give you bad shudders,
Smothered, outnumbered, they dive-bomb your bowl,
Dessert is deserted, blame the Flying Patrol,
Fantastic tactics, all flies equipped
With a first-class flying certificate.
Bubba Bluebottle, swagger fly,
Throwin' da shapes wid da moosic on high,
Doin' ah rap, expressing concerns,
Spreading many dreaded, decrepit germs!

04 August 2019 21:23

Tale of a Pregnant Teapot

***

"The tea-pot is pregnant again!"
Said the jug,
Hot water is needed for the birth,
The mid-wife kettle was there in seconds
As a hospital tended by a nurse!

The tea-pot felt flustered,
Almost flipped her lid
Feeling her temperature rise,
She felt rather drawn as her offspring were born
From embryo tea bags inside!

"Aren't they lovely,
Fresh and bubbly!"
Remarked a china side-plate,
Three fine cups of tea steaming proudly,
Sugar lumps dumped to celebrate!

Doilies agreed,
"They look so sweet!
Identical triplets indeed!
A stirring moment to savour the flavour,
A blend of splendid caffeine!"

Two fine sons, adequately strong,
A daughter of exquisite taste,
Like mother, devout but not up the spout

She was poured through in this case!

"They're an asset! All three!
Just my cup of tea!"
The tablecloth decreed in gleeful splendour,
"I'm not one to stir, I've seen tea inferior
That makes throats choke;
A tongue extender!"

Before it was ravished
A cucumber sandwich
Anguished that tea was a strain
But viewed these three as a delicacy,
An exception to her claim!

A butter dish took advantage
Spreading rumours
Across the table,
"Don't butter them up,
It's not the tea it's the cups
That make resistance incapable!"

Whether you object
To this selective subject
It's absolutely plain
You can see the signs that signify
The tea-pot's pregnant again!

***

Talons and Talents

***

Trees, fields, greenery revealed;
Leaves of a symmetry, waterproof shield,
Cuticle covered, wax protection,
Dripping drops from a storm descension,
Battered by winds, quivering stems,
Shaking, flaking flower stamens,
Baubles of raindrops after the storm
Transparent by nature, perfectly formed,
Gathering weight as they roll into one
Gaining speed as a bullet from a gun,
The air smells cleansed, pure and fresh
Showered, deodorised, dried, caressed,
Revitalised, inspired for another day
To accommodate wildlife, instigate change,
Bees, dragonflies, wasps, dry moths
Are feed for birds as they fly across,
Needs are such, breeds survive
On hunting each other to keep alive,
Lush vegetation, shelter for those
From hungry predators searching for food,
Frogs, toads, elastic tongues
Snatch their prey with a hint of fun,
That pause, delay, sudden strike,
Deadly precision timed just right,
The swoop of an eagle, a kestrel's hover,
Timing is essence, no question of cover,
Sharp teeth, strong beaks, the closing of claws,

The talons and talents of predators
Passed onto their youngsters
Gifted the same
Perks of certain species maintained,
Evolving, revolving in a relay, a sprint
Assuring avoidance of becoming extinct,
The collusion of evolution cuts through like a knife
Let's salute the renewals, the circle of life!

13 March 2023 09:49

Teddy Bear Story

***

Promiscuous Teddy
Kissed the dolls;
He had a reputation,
Was never racist,
Loved them all:
Chinese, black or Asian!

Promiscuous Teddy
Pouted his lips,
Looked so debonair,
Walked rather camp
With an outstretched hand,
Never wore underwear!

Promiscuous Teddy
Willing & ready,
Could not get enough,
He stroked Cindy`s waist,
She slapped his face,
Told him to "get stuffed!"

Promiscuous Teddy
Bedded the dolls
Seduced by a cuddly bear,
He held them close,
They gave him a dose
Of Toy Shop Gonorrhoea!

Promiscuous Teddy
Played with toys,
Enjoyed the opposite sex,
During bondage
It all went wrong
Ted broke his fucking neck!

The Adventures of Cartoon Boy

***

A "think bubble" grows,
Hovers over his head;
Cartoon Boy with street cred,
Cap on backwards,
Flavourless gum,
Mp3 player full on,
Dressed in T-shirt,
Pumps and shorts,
Up to antics, sometimes caught,
Features weekly on page six,
Conjures mischief, plunders tricks,
Loves his Terrier; Mister Spoon,
Rescued from a Rescue Home,
Oddly named, aptly right,
Called that as he stirs at night.
Cartoon Boy does a paper round,
Delivering all through Cartoon Town,
Nancy Freckles pecks his cheek
As he rides his bike down Sketching Street,
Hurdling fences, jumping gates,
Trampling gardens, more complaints,
"There he is! It's all his fault!
That imbecile with a catapult!"
Smashing windows, damaging vases,
Running off in fits of laughter,
Tying girls' pony-tails
On the buses, never fails,

Worms in pockets, bugs in hair,
Creepy-crawlies everywhere,
Cartoon Boy obsessed with pranks
Leaves rubber ducks on river banks,
Sprays, "No Graffiti!" on the wall
And, "Humpty Dumpty had a fall!"
He enters shops, squashes crisps,
Flattens muffins with his fist,
Punctures condoms with a pin,
Loosens lids on air-tight tins,
Lets down tyres of random cars,
Treads on gardens full of flowers,
Slugs are slid through letter boxes,
Stink bombs dropped, the stench obnoxious,
Water cups above the door
Designed to soak, provoke, deplore,
Banana skins guarantee fate;
Victim's whipped arse over face,
A pound coin glued in the middle of the road,
Pedestrians stop, it can't be removed,
Locks blocked with superglue,
Who's responsible, is it you?
Cartoon Boy delights his readers,
Makes them chuckle, giggles, pleases,
Has adventures every week,
Pencilled-in in Sketching Street,
Causing mayhem, getting "lip"
From characters in the comic strip,
Agitated, so annoyed
By practical jokes of
Cartoon Boy!

The Annual Doggie Dinner Dance

***

The meal went fine
Washed down with white wine,
Brussels sprouts trod in the carpet,
Gravy stains on shirts and ties,
Open flies (something to laugh at),
Chocolate mints, wafer thin
For that after-dinner taste,
You shouldn't touch the pudding
If you're slimming down your waist!
Drinks served at the Function Bar
Overpriced, not cheap,
An intoxicated pensioner
Leans on the wall asleep,
Tables are cleared, tips are shared,
Waitresses work fast,
A cheeky, inebriated stranger
Nips bums as they pass,
The crescendo of noise gets louder,
People shout so others can hear,
The disco lights start flashing,
Dancers bop a lot, shake their rears
Performing personal dance routines,
Solo or in pairs
While friends sip their alcohol
Discussing wild affairs,
As if by a freak of nature
'Dirty Dancing' began to play,

The floor had cleared, most disappeared,
One couple gladly stayed,
She was thirty years his junior,
Blonde hair, full of life,
They looked oddball, most peculiar,
Not suited as man and wife,
As the music raised its tempo
She threw herself about,
Wiggling her most tender parts
That threatened to fall out,
He had no style or rhythm
Running to catch her up,
She strutted round the dance floor
While he was fit to drop,
She made him feel years younger,
An agile, able stud
But he resembled a wilted flower,
She, a meagre bud,
It was the annual doggie dinner dance,
The owners were on parade,
First prize to our Dirty Dancers
For best laugh of the day!

The Art of a Cunning Lyricist

***

She's humming a tune never heard before,
Her mind plays games working out the chords,
'La-la-ing' lyrics that don't exist;
The art of a cunning lyricist!

Plucking the strings of her acoustic guitar,
Sat on a stool in a coffee bar,
She's a regular customer allowed the perk,
Down on her luck, out of work!

Fingers on the fretboard, thinking out loud,
Strumming a tune despite the crowd,
No-one listens while sipping their brew,
Familiar faces, usual crew!

A cigarette break, breath of fresh air,
She watches people, tries not to stare,
Finds inspiration, words that rhyme,
Her musical jigsaw fitting fine!

Scribbling notes on a wrinkled pad,
Not upbeat but kind of sad,
Boy meets girl but one of them strays,
Temptations in that early phase!

Into music, acoustic songs,
Her choice to choose what she's playing on,

The raw bare-bones of a solo singer,
One instrument; one sure-shot winner!

She juggles the words to ensure they fit,
Song writing is so intricate,
When finished will be one to treasure,
Personalised but shared together!

She's humming a tune never heard before,
No-one listens, she's just ignored,
A few more tweaks, the song will exist;
The art of a cunning lyricist!

20 May 2023 13:51

The Belly-Button Tree

***

Gather round children, go secretly
Through the Twenty Acre Wood
To the Belly-Button Tree, admission is free,
it's in your neighbourhood,
Stand in line, form an orderly queue
There's a wooden belly-button you can step through,
Sit on the slide it will take you down
To the sound of music on a merry-go-round,
Astride a horse or a unicorn,
Wave to the crowd the music has drawn,
Toffee-apples held on a slick, thick stick,
Don't eat on the rides or you might feel sick,
Candy floss hanging where you hook a duck,
A prize every time with a stroke of luck,
There's a ghost train ride in the absolute dark,
Sinister voices put on for a lark,
A maze of mirrors to confuse the brain,
Rides in the 'park' on a miniature train,
Bungee jumping from an elevated crane,
Supervised firing at a toy rifle range,
Pinball machines, the 'two-penny roll';
A pay out should coins land in a row,
There's fun in sport; a three-legged race,
Coming last is no disgrace,
Apple bobbing; water up nose,
The gasping for breath, wetted clothes,
Ping pong tournaments, basketball nets,

Skipping ropes, hoops around necks,
Joy and laughter for happy kids,
The venue, a secret; location, well hid.
Gather round children, go hurriedly
Through the Twenty Acre Wood
To the Belly-Button Tree, excitedly,
I recommend you should,
It's exclusive, elusive, relatively new,
There's a wooden belly-button you can step through!

20 May 2022 20:00

The Bonnie Bauble Affair

***

Hooray! the lid is open,
Eventually lifted off,
Torch light seems too bright,
It's so dark in this loft,
Stuck here throughout the whole year
With tinsel for the tree,
Hiding like an illegal refugee!

Down the step ladder
Into the front room,
All sorts, assorted baubles,
Multi-coloured balloons,
I sit in my tray
Among its cardboard casing,
Waiting with other Christmas decorations!

The tree is in place,
We all want to be selected,
Admired, desired,
Not neglected or rejected,
Bauble Bonnie is a honey,
We've been together for a year,
Stored away for Christmas
As a matching pair!

Fumbling fingers pick us,
Lift us out of the box,

We're scrutinised by inquisitive eyes
To be utilised, maybe not!
Relieved, we're hung on the nearest branch
To be part of the festive spree,
But I mustn't look up the angel's dress
On top of the tree above me!

We hear all conversations,
Scandal, dramatic affairs,
How the vicar ran off with so-and-so
Midway through morning prayers,
His mistress is a chatterbox,
Never rests her tongue,
Talks non-stop till heads drop,
God help him from now on!

Christmas time is especially fine,
A period I treasure,
While Bonnie Bauble's on the tree
We hang around together,
We're reflected in a decorative way,
Our lacquered finish is superb;
She can see herself in me,
I can see myself in her!

The fairy lights are quite a sight,
Twinkling off and on,
Twelve cans of lager
Vanish without a magic wand,
The old man in the armchair
Swigging back the beer,
Soon he'll find he'll be inclined
To make it reappear!

Grandad's hogged the tv remote,
No-one wants to get up,
The 3-piece is so cosy,
Full of bums and a dozing pup,
The Queen's Speech is soon over,
Toffee wrappers on the carpet,
Sick drama on Eastenders,
Wallace And Gromit to laugh at!

Overload of stomachs with food,
Everyone's feeling the strain,
Drinking the drinks that shouldn't be drunk
Then off to the loo again,
Outside if you dare for a breath of fresh air
Or a fag for that nicotine fix
As drunks stagger by
Shouting carols to the sky,
Giving wheelie-bins a good kick!

Friends and family kiss at the door
Saying, "Thanks for Christmas dinner!"
Tucking in scarves, buttoning coats
Against the chill of winter,
Uncle Fizz had soft drinks,
(Short-straw drawn for driving),
While others had a tipple or two
Even before arriving!

There's custard down the table leg,
Nut shells underneath,
Left-over gateaux licked by the cat who's
Too fat for a cat's physique,
Tea stains left on armchairs,
Celery leaves by the bin,

Christmas celebrations of drinking and tasting,
A case of unashamed self-indulging!

It's great to hear laughter,
The occasional moan
From family and friends
Combined in one home,
Christmas, mistletoe kisses,
Gentle heating of mulled wine,
The chinking of glasses, pleasantries passed
While clasping a drink of some kind!

Christmas time is so sublime,
A personal joy forever,
Bonnie Bauble next to me,
Hanging around together,
I have L O on my chest,
Etched in gold, italic flair,
She has V E, conveniently,
To confirm we're a matching pair!

The Chemotherapy Cavalry

***

These are the dumb, do-nothing days
Spent staring at walls in a whimsical haze,
Grounded by cancer tormenting my neck
Chemotherapy-remedy after effects,
The nocturnal wakening, spitting of phlegm,
Sipping of water; an endless trend,
The thumping of pillows, grumbling alone,
Wondering if cancer has whittled or grown,
Insane mind games, no clues for three months,
After tests the assessment; progress or stumped,
Your life in the hands of an internal intrusion
Portraying arrogance, body-abusing,
Polluting the system, choosing to kill
Any vulnerable organs on principal,
Causing mayhem, ruling the roost,
Contrived, epitomised, since introduced,
An enemy marching, bayonets attached,
Cowards' confrontation; no defence, just attack,
A one-way callous onslaught. malice, indignity
Interrupted by the induction of the chemotherapy cavalry,
Swashbuckling combat, muskets at the ready,
The battlefield is actually staged within my belly,
Small room to manoeuvre, aggression face to face,
Ferocity is proven, hostility embraced,
A clash of two aggressors both stubborn to a degree;
Cancer versus the worst of the chemotherapy cavalry!

01 February 2023 11:58

The Coughalot Club

***

Tissues are an issue,
Can't get enough
When you're a member
Of The Coughalot Club,
Sneezes, wheezes,
Seizures of breath,
An intake of cold air
Has maximum effect,
Your tonsils; a punch-bag
For sparring germs,
Skipping with strings
Of phlegm you've churned,
In knee-length,
Snot-drenched boxing shorts,
(No gum "shield"
From the cold you've caught!)
"Seconds out! Round one!"
You're fighting Symptom,
An experienced ailment
That batters your system,
Dodging blows of the nose,
Watery vision,
No joke, sore throat,
Duck and dive collisions
When Symptom comes at you
To upset your health
You need protection,

Defend yourself,
Hear the bell?
The first Round is over,
A brief reprieve from
Common Cold hangovers!

Squinty eyes, half normal size,
Blood-shot, strained, veined,
Bulging when convulsing
With a pupil-popping plague,
Brought on by a moron tickling,
Prickling itching throats,
Harassing the larynx
With uncharitable chokes,
Health in the Red Corner
Versus Snot Kid in the Blue,
Below the belt punches
In a viral, frantic mood,
Ten Rounds scheduled
To determine the result,
No excuses if Health loses
It`s the Snot Kid`s fault!
Keep the spotlight on them
As it`s well into the night,
The outcome could prove vital
As a Health issue highlight,
Points are gained on merit,
Efforts to outwit
The opponent during moments
When defences slip a bit,
An uppercut to the windpipe,
A calamity, damaging punch.
Inhalation inhibited,
Lungs deflated at once,

The immune system going down
Under a quick "one-two",
Lost control, knocked out cold
Defeated by cheating flu!

Every year colds reappear
We share the sticky stuff,
Reluctant, elected members
Of the Coughalot Club!
Hawking in libraries,
Being told to "shush",
Reader's tutting, fussing;
Can't concentrate on books,
Oh no! you have no handkerchief!
That tingle in your nose
Is mingling with mischief,
Ready to explode,
You look around frantically
For a corner out of the way,
Your uncontrolled, desperate sneeze
Creates great overspray,
Your chunder sounds like thunder,
Startled witnesses stand back,
Afraid to catch the impact
Of your nasal-spray attack,
Waiting at the bus-stop,
Stifling sniffing sounds,
You climb the stairs to the upper deck,
The following queue stay down,
The phone rings, you answer it,
Demands upon your voice,
Talk turns into coughing fits
Of which you have no choice,
Sympathy, consequently,

There's never, ever enough
Especially for long-term members
Of the Coughalot Club!

The Floral Sacrifice

***

How could I forget you?
One thing I can't ignore
'Who stole the bunch of flowers
I left outside your door?'
A token of affection
Undetected, unobserved
The card I wrote in its envelope;
You never read a single word!

'Try not to take it personally'
Is what friends say to me,
The whole affair is certainly
My main priority,
I appreciate the close concern;
You learn from sound advice
This situation irritates:
The floral sacrifice!

How could I ever neglect you?
Your intellect demands more,
'Who stole the bunch of flowers
I left outside your door?'
A symbol of devotion,
Declaration of intent,
The words I wrote in my two-line note
Were well and truly meant!

THE FLORAL SACRIFICE

A violation of privacy,
Sabotage of a personal kind,
An intrusion leaving bruising
On a sentimental mind,
Once is sorely bad enough
To pay the ultimate price
It's a matter of principle;
The floral sacrifice!

How could it not affect you?
The unexpected was in store,
'Who stole the bunch of flowers
I left outside your door?'
Intended as a big surprise
With you arriving home,
My two-line verse, uncoerced
Now certainly unknown!

Put biting lips, regrets aside
I'll try to even the score,
'Who stole the bunch of flowers
I left outside your door?'
Next time I'll tread more carefully,
No need for stress and cursing;
I'll read the verse well-rehearsed
In person!

02 July 2022 20:12

The Forest of Dreams

***

Lincoln Green can be seen in the Forest of Dreams,
A supreme camouflage for leprechauns,
In traditional tunics, they love Irish music,
Rise at the breaking of dawn,
Busy themselves by cracking shells
Of seeds from chestnut trees,
They fish in the lake where no humans partake
Dangling their rods in the reeds!

The air is so clean in the Forest of Dreams,
Hear the swish of gossamer wings,
The flight of the Fantail Fairy
With her precarious mood swings,
Collecting settled dew drops
From smooth and nettled leaves,
She lets them slide inside
Her waiting water-pot with ease!

Surreal and serene in the Forest of Dreams,
Unblemished by menace or man,
Nature in its natural state;
Unscathed: as originally planned,
Bluebirds chirping nonstop
Nonchalantly sweet,
Quaint, unique, compact physique,
Petite with nimble beaks!

Bubbles in streams in the Forest of Dreams,
Leprechaun children weaving baskets,
Happily chatting while interacting
With wicker techniques and fasteners,
The Master Baker making bread
In an unorthodox manner,
Loaves and rolls so everyone's fed
With energy, fibre and stamina!

Lettuce and beans in the Forest of Dreams,
Cauliflowers, cabbages, leeks,
Green fingers of leprechaun gardeners
Contrast with rosy-red cheeks,
Busy-bees hum in flower heads
Selecting nectar stored in sacs,
Pollen in hindleg baskets
Complete the floral act!

Romantic scenes in the Forest of Dreams;
Leprechauns kissing fairies,
Babies born in dry weather or storms,
The climate seems so varied,
Thank heaven the landscape has good soil
Unspoiled by human presence,
The Forest of Dreams is basically
Home to the current residents!

24 November 2022 21:14

The Home-Town Rats

***

Ears twitching, nostrils sniffing,
Swishing of the tail,
These rodent rats search wishing
For scraps along the trail,
Scratching at bin liners,
Tearing polythene bags,
Pawing dirty nappies,
Used condoms, smoked fags,
Hoping for titbits, half eaten food;
A discarded McNuggets
With fries half chewed,
A carved chicken carcass
With slithers of meat;
A thrown-away takeaway
Left on a seat,
A portion of chips
Unwrapped and dropped,
Salt and vinegared
From the chip shop,
A peeled banana,
Out-of-date cream
Tinned, binned
For the sake of hygiene,
Anything edible,
A family to feed
Nesting somewhere
In the vicinity,

Surviving, multiplying,
Spreading disease,
Running amok,
Doing as they please,
Heartily partying,
Free from parole
Getting high inhaling
Squirts from cans of aerosols,
Illegal all-night raves,
Misbehaving despite advice
Whenever entertaining
They should be quiet as mice,
There's always someone somewhere
Who's bound to smell a rat,
If one should dare appear
You want to squash the fucker flat,
It's better to ignore it
For it will not bite or scratch ya,
Leave it to professionals;
The impressionable rat catcher,
These flea infested immigrants
Never pay rent,
Council tax is free of charge,
They crap to their heart's content,
Resemble Rod Stewart
With their nose the main event,
I don't suppose they karaoke
If you do then you could text me,
Just think...a half-pissed swaying rat
Singing 'Do Ya Think I'm Sexy?'
Meanwhile, down the drainpipes
Seeking this and that
The uninvited immigrants;
The Home-town Rats

Gigging in your garden,
Digging up the dirt,
The males don't wear trousers,
Females, no skirts,
They're a law unto themselves
That is, unless we lay some traps
To catch the little buggers;
The Home-town Rats!

05 March 2023 20:05

The Honeybee-Buzz

***

He's got the honeybee-buzz 'cause he loves you,
The sting from every cocktail glass,
Half a dozen by your elbow bear your fingerprints,
In his wallet lies your portrait photograph!

He's got the honeybee-buzz from your aura,
The story of a male head over heels,
A one-way love; real, not a bluff,
Spinning on a roulette wheel!

He's got the honeybee-buzz in a frenzy
With plenty of spare testosterone,
You're the queen of his angst, his jealousy,
The target for his disheartened drone!

He's got the honeybee-buzz in his pocket,
A locket with a strand of your hair,
This total obsession isn't lessening,
It's a solo event he'd like to share!

He's got the honeybee-buzz from your perfume;
A musky scent left hanging in the room,
Your socialising level is rising,
He retires with exposed rejection wounds!

17 February 2023 17:14

The Pope

***

The Pope
Wears a
Ceremonious cloak,
He's declared
By a vote
And white
Smoke,
He hails
From the Vatican
Wearing that flat
Hat again; a
Latin-speaking,
Roman Catholic
Bloke!

The Silent Cemetery

***

Walk among the gravestones,
Here lies a man in peace;
Elijah Bone, his headstone
Between the moss reads 'Priest',
Nineteen-ten to fifty-two,
What fatality did he suffer?
A holy figure in the ground
Heaven bound like any other!

Mary May, the doctor's wife
Died of acute pneumonia,
No treatment can defeat or beat
Conditions that control you,
John Thomson lay six feet away
Also six feet down,
It's said they buried him
Straight from bed
Still in his dressing gown!

Laura Whittock, film critic,
Died in a cinema seat,
Had a heart attack sat at the back
While sucking a lozenge sweet,
Simon Ziar handled wires
As all electricians do,
Five thousand volts made him jolt,
Smoked his boiler suit!

Emily Bron, a veterinarian,
Performed operations on pets,
Her sneeze caused alarm,
Jerking her arm;
She stabbed herself in the vest,
Arthur Creek, a chimney sweep
Covered in thick, black soot
Was hit at night by a motorbike
As he crossed the road on foot!

Simon Pane felt framed,
A double-glazing rep
Was double-crossed by a client
Who claimed they'd both had sex,
Her husband got to hear of this,
Shot him in the back,
Simon's eyes were double-glazed
As a company Pane collapsed!

Moira Tucket, concussed by a bucket
Led to her being deceased,
She looked rather pale
When the ambulance came;
Whiter than the whitest sheet,
Bill Cumberton, rather cumbersome,
Fell into a river while fishing,
Never surfaced, his breath was worthless
As fresh air was definitely missing!

Agnes Beard did a parachute jump
In aid of her favourite charity,
Unlike many she fell in the cemetery,
Buried there, causing hilarity,

Margaret Strife, the undertaker's wife
Tripped over a random poodle,
Fell awkwardly, died at the scene,
Had a discount on her funeral!

Jeremy Jarvis could dance so well
He would spin a pirouette,
Unprovoked he had a stroke,
Danced his last Quick Step,
Michelle Tibs. a librarian,
Was climbing high, steep steps,
Slipped and tumbled headfirst
From a shelf on 'Seek Safe Sex'!

Brian, the psycho sci-fi bod
Died of natural causes,
Reported sightings of UFOs,
Several flying saucers,
Suzie Sexton, up all night,
Entertained the men,
Deflated, suffocated
By a thirty stone African!

Linda Moy loved hiking,
Packed her red rucksack,
Leaned over a cliff edge
To view laid eggs,
Forgot to stop, lean back,
Simon Dredge, on Safari,
A nostalgic collector of stamps,
Photographed giraffes in the path
Of stampeding elephants!

Walk among the gravestones,

A varied list of guests
Share the silent cemetery
When eventually laid to rest,
Characters from all walks of life
Unknowingly together,
Remembered with sincerity
By friends et cetera!

The Welcomed Arrival of Spring

***

Put the clocks forward for earlier dawns,
Roll out bright sunshine on newly cut lawns,
Days have been far too dark and dull;
Winter behaves in a subdued lull,
Crack open champagne, toast the warmth seeping in,
The welcomed arrival of spring!

As we lose sixty minutes of precious time
The hands of old clocks perform a rewind,
Summertime in Britain, a fitting reprieve
From shivering, shaking, shuddering freeze,
Optimism bubbles, doubles everything;
The welcomed arrival of spring!

Early birds catch the illustrious worm,
If days aren't fulfilled you need to be firm,
Slide out of bed to the promising day,
More hours to devour, advantage gained,
Throw back the curtains, hear morning-birds sing,
The welcomed arrival of spring!

Another day, another dollar, swallow your pride,
Take the bull by the horns don't be bashful or shy,
Confidence promises better returns,
Reap what you sow, absorb what you learn,
Tomorrow you can wallow, allowing in
The welcomed arrival of spring!

At last! vivid colours to photograph,
The black and white winter is in the past,
Open-neck shirts, miniscule skirts,
Lollipops licked to quench the thirst,
Bodies sunbathing to tinge the skin,
The welcomed arrival of spring!

23 March 2023 10:56

Toy-Box Scenario

***

"I love you One-Eyed Teddy!"
Ragdoll whispers in his ear,
She squeezes his paw with passion,
Sports a smile from ear to ear,
Rubs his bruised arm gently,
Abused in a recent fight;
A tussle with pouting Panda
Over frantic girlfriend rights,
"I sat with Ragdoll in the toy-box,
Kissed her under the mistletoe!"
One-Eyed Teddy bellowed,
"YES! nine months ago!"
Panda takes a deep breath
As all stuffed animals do,
(It`s a closely guarded secret
They breathe like me and you),
Lanky Giraffe sticks his neck out,
"Why can`t we all be friends?
Shake paws, ignore trivialities,
Be cuddly, comforting!"
Fur Fox loves to stir things,
Friction is his middle name,
Wry, sly, devious,
Lets others take the blame,
Jumbles finished jigsaws,
Wrecks board games, hides the dice,
Ties skipping ropes together,

Breaks springs of clockwork mice,
Pentagon the Policeman
Tries to catch him at it,
Hides inside a cardboard box,
Fur Fox decides to flatten it!
Maisy and Mollie Dollies;
Twins who're always together,
Where one goes the other shows
As birds always with feathers,
Ring A Ring O Roses,
Dancing, singing songs,
Happy, carefree laughing days,
Children sing along,
Montague the Monkey
Lacks access to tall trees,
Scratches artificial fibres
For imaginary fleas,
Petulant Puppet Pinocchio
Spreads so many lies,
His tell-tale nose doesn't grow
But his belly does with pies,
Celibate Pink Elephants
If ever seen can't harm us,
Witnessed periodically by
Drinking Karl Koala,
Minnie Mop does the washing
In her pinafore, rubber gloves,
Irons fab clothes for Barbie Dolls,
Ken's suits, shirt collars, cuffs,
Pooch Pug-Pup Penny
Plays with perky Penelope Puss,
Toy cats and dogs are compatible,
No animosity or fuss,
Willy Worm, made from Afghan wool

TOY-BOX SCENARIO

Is a colourful six-inch length,
Talks in Lewis Carroll riddles
Making very little sense,
Building Bricks keep falling down,
Someone's having fun,
Baby Badger's happy
As he taps the bottom ones,
Glove Puppet Sooty,
A favourite with kids,
Never said, "Izzy whizzy!"
Matthew Corbett did,
Lego Bricks, all sizes mixed,
Tossed across the floor and hall,
Trips up dolls and animals
In horizontal falls,
Piles of toys, fur lined, annoyed,
Trip over random blocks,
Bump into one another
Recovering from knocks,
Tempers flare on occasions,
Rottweiler Ronnie shouts,
"Don't sniff my butt Boxer Pup,
I'll knock your stuffing out!"
Endless tenderness,
Moments of warm bliss,
Doll's heads on vacant shoulders,
Signs of sentimental solace,
One-Eyed Teddy cuddles Ragdoll
In a romantic interlude,
"I love you gorgeous gumdrop!"
"Teddy! I love you too!"

Tremor

***

The sky with a face like thunder
Growling at the earth below,
Spitting sprays of threatening rain
Before the downpour flows!

With a darkening mood of menace
Black clouds gather ranks,
A whiplash of lightening flash
Shows anger in the angst!

Rumbles of discontentment
Resentment and remorse
Are typified by troubled skies
As do soldiers suffering wars!

There's bitterness in sharp winds,
Sarcasm as it bites,
The north wind is critical, cynical,
Typically impolite!

The wrath of thunder deafens
As the heavens open wide,
People at sixes and sevens
Desperate to get inside!

Hostility stirs in the atmosphere
From a stratosphere of fear,

An intrusion of confusion
In a whirlwind riled affair!

Feel torment in what's overhead,
An incredible strength of might,
The twisting, turning of currents
In a frantic ferocious fight!

The devil, red with violence
As the sky is lit in the storm,
A rage that chases silence
Into a subdued form!

Clouds with traces of thunder
Intimidate the earth below,
Overcome with strain, cascades of rain
As whipping wild winds blow!

24 February 2023 07:41

Two Stars out of Six

***

Leaving me while sleeping
Was a wake-up call,
The final stage,
An unrehearsed play
Before the curtain fall,
I failed to read the unwritten script,
Had to ad lib it all,
Your acting skills
Have been fulfilled,
Will there be an encore?

Talk about surprises!
This arrived wildly
Out of the blue,
A deceptive, rejected,
Effective objective,
Unexpected move,
I thought we were compatible,
I'm apparently overruled,
Deceived in total complacency,
Too late to see
The truth!

Been there, done it,
There's no fun in it,
Didn't think it would happen again,
Deja vu,

A repetitive clue,
Feeling similar
If not the same,
Losing my touch
With the ladies
Feels like money lost
Down a drain,
My Casanova-manoeuvres
Need improving,
Outdated with age.

Actions speak louder than words,
They left me speechless when you'd gone,
You'd actually scored a victory
Making me history,
Moving on,
Life's a gamble, a mystery,
There are losers,
Those who've won,
Beggars can't be choosers
So ...so long!

War of Words

***

The falling in, the falling out,
The niggles plus those nagging doubts,
Rising rages built on hate
Increased by anger, escalate,
Fuels the fire for high-raised voices,
A few choice words (unfortunate choices),
Accusations crude and lewd
While tackling factual points of view,
Disputes to choose the truth is strong,
Drawing conclusions, arguing on,
No happy medium, tedium strikes,
Long droll days, humdrum nights,
Hours that while our lives away
In hot discussions, blinding rage,
Shouting matches, volume high,
Loud hoarse voices parched and dry,
Whispers have no place where there
Is such an intense atmosphere,
Pointing fingers, proportioning blame,
Calling one another names,
Insults from mouths spitting phlegm,
Gritted teeth in unison,
Hot-heads embedded in disagreements
Dread a sequence of regretted grievance,
Momentary silence suffered inside,
A pause for breath to energize,
Looks of resentment, stares of contempt,

A war of words less compliments,
A concentrate of stalemate, puff for puff;
Tit for tat, enough is enough,
Conclusion disillusion, arms outspread,
A gesture of innocence being misled,
Apologies frivolity; none on the agenda,
A reservation stating 'return to sender ',
Chock-a-block, progression locked, cul-de-sac dead end,
Closure to the whole debate is hard to comprehend,
Settlement is detriment, festers on the side,
Rest assured to raise its head with a pledge undignified,
The war of words is a verbal curse in any shape or form,
A defence against the relentlessness
Of being right or wrong!

13 May 2023 09:15

Water Baby

***

Water Baby christened with glistening oil,
Welcome to Fresh Water World,
The bubbling under of fish-world wonder;
The flushes, the gushes, the swirls!

Your maiden swim in the aquarium;
Your river of future dreams
To explore with raw delirium
Refreshed in constant streams!

Pause only to rest although obsessed
By an eager intrigue to learn,
A new-born facing trials and tests
With interest, enquired concerns!

Currents so strong spur you on
Invigorate, stimulate, strengthen,
Emulate heat from the burning sun
As summer days lazily lengthen!

Between coarse reeds you swim with ease,
The ability bestowed from birth,
Twists and turns, the agility;
Priceless in its worth!

Precaution before exhaustion,
The need to return to 'the nest'

Reunited with brothers and sisters
In a family conquest!

08 May 2023 08:43

Wedding Day

***

Good luck to the bride
Good luck to the groom,
Once divided, united,
Marrying soon,
Vows to stay loyal,
Oaths of faith
Prone to be tested
At later dates,
A life together
Through thick and thin
Thriving on
Driven adrenalin,
Running a house,
Keeping a home
Cosy and comfy
Like Darby and Joan,
Sharing chores,
Meals for two;
The sofa at night
When day is through,
A low-lit room
In a chilled-out mood,
Laid-back music
Lulls and soothes,
Relaxes, enacts with
Melancholy moods,
Occasionally a brazen

Lover's tiff;
Voices raised
As the volume lifts,
Harsh words hurt,
Accusations fly,
Arguments fade
To a whimper and die,
A temporary break-up
With make-up to follow,
Non-returnable verbal's
Hard to swallow,
Hugs, embraces
Replace torment;
Faces relieved,
Pleased, content,
Peace restored,
Calm prevails,
Their relationship
Stays on the rails,
Full steam ahead
On the right track
A minor glitch
With minimal impact,
It's the customary baggage
Which comes with the ride
Sometimes leans badly
On the heavy side,
The balance required
Evens things out,
Goodbye to the stinging,
Lingering doubt,
Hello to elation;
The raise, the lift,
That excited sensation,

The encouragement it gives,
A flourish to already
Reddened cheeks,
Coloured by
An optimistic streak,
The cherished harmony
Of woman and man,
A solid foundation
For making plans,
First, the engagement;
The couple betrothed
The wedding arrangement;
Hands to hold,
A bold decision,
Life-changing act,
Highly important
Not matter-of-fact,
The joining together
Of two as one
On a journey
Eternally second to none.
Good luck to the groom,
Good luck to the bride
Their wedding day
Has finally arrived!

23 October 2021 18:41

White Stick

***

Blind man tapping a white stick
Testing where not to walk,
Resting on street corners
So as not to get overawed,
His disability plain to see
He takes it all in his stride,
Some help with his inadequacy,
Others pass him by,
A partially-sighted person
Braving busy roads,
Aided by those conscious
He may not make it home,
A strive for independence,
Venturing out alone,
Unafraid to face threats
That may prove a fatal blow,
Known by nearby retailers
(Cheerful, cheery chat),
They fetch him what he wants in store,
Get him this and that,
Discussions concerning headlines,
Jokes about the weather,
Pokes at tv actors;
Amateurish, not clever,
He has a sense of humour,
Not obvious from his appearance,
Concentration taking over,

His expression, rather serious,
He crosses the road, traffic slows
With understanding patience,
The white stick signals hardship
Regarding simple operations,
He calls in at the cafe,
Settles in his favourite seat,
The one by the window
Where the nets don't quite meet,
He smells the frying bacon,
Has an all-day breakfast meal,
Salt and vinegar gently shaken,
Tomato sauce completes the deal,
Steaming tea, two welcomed 'sugars',
A round of buttered bread;
A satisfying meal indeed
To face the day ahead,
More banter with the waitress,
Flirtatious, smiling, warm,
On first name terms with customers,
Her uniform quite worn,
"Have a good day, Sonny!"
She clears the cluttered table,
He takes his waiting white stick,
"The same to you, my Mabel!"
Tapping walls and fences,
Finding open gaps,
Detecting accident pitfalls
That could roll him on his back,
His jolly, upbeat temperament
Deserves a deal of praise,
Restrictions on his abilities
Defied, brushed away,
A strong determination

To make the most of life
Despite an inclination to give in,
Hindered with the handicap of only partial sight
The white stick helps an otherwise loser win!

Winter Wonder

***

They're felling trees to sell as logs,
My, how the bark has grown!
Winds of winter versus timber
Warming chill-filled homes!

Wreaths hung on front doors
With leaves of evergreen
To symbolise invites for Christ
In a Christian cuisine!

Stars top traditional Christmas trees
Or ribbons tied in bows,
Preference is an option
Depends on individuals!

Christmas crackers on the table,
Crackling laid on plates,
Turkey for the omnivores,
Sausages and steak!

Tinsel glitters under lightbulbs,
Baubles sparkle on the tree,
Mistletoe is hung for those
Who're on a kissing spree!

Invitations for parties,
Exchanging Christmas gifts,

Pleasantries put minds at ease
At the time they need a 'lift'!

Granddaughters perched on grandma's knee
Reciting Christmas carols,
Grandad dressed as Santa Clause
In all the red apparel!

Mince pies on ceramic plates,
Heated sausage rolls,
Cocktail sticks with sausages pricked,
Snacks in various bowls!

Raise a glass of mulled wine,
Take a soothing sip,
Mix the taste of pate'
With the guacamole dip!

Here comes that suspicious tradition
Where 'Merry Christmas' should be banned
So as not to offend religions
Imported from foreign lands!

Kids are building snowmen
Celebrating the season's fall,
Sledging down the icy slopes
In a fun-filled free-for-all!

06 December 2021 21:32

Your Spoken Words

***

Being rude is truly not my intent,
I love your speech impediment,
The way you can't pronounce your 'Es-es'
Announced as a stream of appealing 'yehtheth',
It gives you top notoriety,
Though some may mock its novelty,
Treat you as a source of fun
To hear those words all spoken wrong,
'Chrithmuth Withiuss' leaves me weak,
Undeniably you, so unique!

It wouldn't be you to the same extent
Without your speech impediment,
Your writing doesn't give a clue,
Your 'say' reads 'say' not 'thay' as lips do,
'Path me the thauth pleath' is how you would ask,
'The meal wath delithess, now thwarberry tart,
I'll help with the dithess, thow apprethiathion,
Dry cupth and thawtherth rinthed in the baython'!

Not pronouncing your 'Es-es' is hard to prevent,
I love your speech impediment,
It's evident some will mock your voice,
Choose to ridicule given the choice,
They're all so trivial, immature,
It's you that matters, the one I prefer,
Chatter to me, let me submerge

In the delicate depths of your spoken words,
Accept this as a compliment
I love your speech impediment!

Afterword

***

Okay folks...there you have it.
I feel adequately humbled you've read my poems.
Hopefully they were met with your approval.
'Word Etchings'...the use of words to form pictures in the mind...it's as simple as that!
Thanks for your time!

Glenn
(August 2023)

***

***

Printed in Great Britain
by Amazon